1962

WHAT A YEAR TO BE BORN!

Written by
Robin Bennett-Freebairn and Joe Toussaint

Published by Emersive
www.whatayeartobeborn.com

What happened in 1962? We all have a special affinity for the year we were born, but how much do we really know about it? This guide takes you through the highs and lows of an historic year towards the end of the baby boom generation. The colour-coded chapters hold a wealth of information that bring you closer to what life was like in this milestone year.

Contents

▶ Introduction

Those born in 1962 were among the last to be a part of the post-war population bulge which defined children born between 1946 and 1964 as "Baby Boomers." The year was embryonic for Britain. It saw the first single, *Love Me Do*, by the Beatles and the first live performance by the Rolling Stones, at the Marquee Jazz Club in London. In the USA, President John F. Kennedy was, unbeknownst to him, in the last full year of his presidency. In Britain, Prime Minister Harold Macmillan dismissed six cabinet members in an unsuccessful attempt to shore up his government. If the Oxford English Dictionary had then, as it does now, a *Word of the Year*, it would have been "cold." The Cold War between America and Russia was at its height; what became known as the Cuban Missile Crisis took the world to the brink of Armageddon. In the UK, a deep freeze set in over the whole of the country in late December and it would not relent until March the following year. It was the harshest winter since 1740.

In sport there were debuts for Geoffrey Boycott at Yorkshire Cricket Club and a first appearance for the most successful golfer in history, Jack Nicklaus, at the (British) Open. In the Football World Cup Final, an injured Pele had to watch from the sidelines as his team, Brazil, beat Czechoslovakia 3-1 to lift the trophy.

In the world of the arts and live performance, Margot Fonteyn and Rudolf Nureyev danced together for the first time in the ballet *Giselle*. David Hockney was in his last year at art college. Half a world away, Andy Warhol was showing how artistic soup cans could be in an exhibition in California. In cinema, the year saw the debut of the quintessentially English spy, James Bond, played by Scotsman Sean Connery in *Dr. No*. Sophia Loren picked up the Best Actress Oscar for her role in *Two Women*, while Maximilian Schell took the prize for Best Actor for *Judgement in Nuremberg*. All of this was overshadowed when, in the early hours of August 5th, Hollywood discovered that it had lost its most precious treasure, Marilyn Monroe. On the small screen *Z-Cars*, *Steptoe and Son*, *The Saint* and *That Was the Week That Was* all debuted.

Immigration from Hong Kong and the Indian subcontinent saw British tastes change so that having a "Chinese" or an "Indian" became a feature of weekly life. As an alternative to plain crisps, a new exotic cheese and onion flavour came on to the market whilst an After Eight mint could be enjoyed as a digestif. The more adventurous home cook would have bought Elizabeth David's *French Provincial Cooking* (published in 1960), which further changed our eating habits. On the road, the new Ford Cortina Mark 1 was the car to be seen in. 1962 also saw a record number of women, 26,000, gain entry to university, giving them greater life choices and fresh impetus to the Women's Liberation Movement.

All in all, the *Swinging Sixties* were well and truly underway.

The Daily Headlines

No: 4943

THREE PENCE

First Edition

Wednesday, January 31, 1962

THE BIG FREEZE TIGHTENS ITS GRIP AS THE COUNTRY GRINDS TO A HALT IN THE COLD

The Daily Headlines

THREE PENCE

Tuesday, July 10, 1962

No: 5103

First Edition

NASA LAUNCHES THE TELSTAR 1 COMMUNICATIONS SATELLITE INTO ORBIT

The Daily Headlines

THREE PENCE

Saturday, August 4, 1962

No: 5128

First Edition

MARILYN MONROE FOUND DEAD IN HER HOTEL ROOM NEXT TO EMPTY MEDICINE BOTTLES

The Daily Headlines

No: 5208

First Edition

THREE PENCE

Tuesday, October 23, 1962

PRESIDENT KENNEDY SIGNS PROCLAMATION AS CUBAN MISSILE CRISIS DEEPENS

Jan 2ⁿᵈ   BBC Television broadcasts the first episode of Z-Cars. Set in the fictional Merseyside town of Newtown, it is seen as a gritty and hard-hitting portrayal of police life.

Jan 3ʳᵈ   Pope John XIII excommunicates Cuban Communist leader Fidel Castro from the Catholic Church.

Jan 4ᵗʰ   The first driverless subway train comes into service carrying passengers in New York between Times Square and Grand Central Station. The journey of less than a mile is chosen to avoid disruption to other services.

Jan 11ᵗʰ   An outbreak of smallpox is recorded in Bradford. A large-scale vaccination programme sees 250,000 people immunised. The emergency is declared over on February 12ᵗʰ. Six deaths are directly linked to the disease.

Jan 11ᵗʰ   An avalanche on Huascarán Mountain in Peru, caused by a sudden rise in temperature, kills more than 4,000 people.

Jan 20ᵗʰ   *Look and Learn* magazine launches. It is an informative and educational publication aimed at the market of younger teenagers. As well as covering subjects as diverse as volcanoes and the Loch Ness Monster, it features a "make a pen-friend" page which encourages readers to make new friends overseas.

Jan 26ᵗʰ   Notorious Mafia mobster Charles "Lucky" Luciano's luck finally runs out when he dies of a heart attack at Naples International Airport.

Feb 4ᵗʰ   The Sunday Times becomes the first British newspaper to print a colour supplement. Entitled *The Sunday Times Colour Section*, it is focusses on fashion with a lead feature of eleven pictures of model Jean Shrimpton wearing a Mary Quant Dress. The photos are by David Bailey.

Feb 5ᵗʰ   There is an extremely rare *Great Conjunction of the Seven Luminaries*; these being the moving astronomical bodies that are visible to the naked eye. The Moon, Mercury, Venus, Mars, Jupiter, Saturn and the Sun were all within 16 degrees of each other. A total solar eclipse is visible in parts of Asia, Australia and the Pacific.

Feb 5th   President John F. Kennedy delivers a Tet (Vietnamese New Year) message to the people of Vietnam and extends his very best wishes for their well-being and the prosperity of the population.

Feb 8th   Nine trade unionists are killed at the instigation of Maurice Papon, the Paris Chief of Police, who had collaborated with the Nazi regime during WW2.

Feb 10th   The convention of dating Acts of Parliament by Monarch's regnal year (the length of time they have been on the throne) comes to an end. Henceforth, acts will be dated by calendar year.

Feb 12th   David Bowie is punched by his old school friend George Underwood during an argument about a girl. He is rushed to London's Moorfields Eye Hospital for emergency surgery on his left eye. Doctors save his vision but his pupil is left permanently dilated.

Feb 13th   A campaign of civil disobedience begins in Wales. In a speech broadcast by the BBC, Welsh Nationalist Saunders Lewis calls on all Welsh speakers to refuse to fill in forms written in English only. The influential pressure group *Cymdeithas yr Iaith Gymraeg* is born.

Feb 16th   The city of Sheffield is hit by hurricane force winds. 4 people are killed and 250 homes are destroyed. There is also substantial damage to the Brammall Lane Stadium, home of Sheffield United football club. The area is declared a national disaster zone, triggering government funding for reparations.

Feb 16th   Flash floods hit the coast of West Germany, killing 315 people and destroying around 60,000 properties.

Feb 20th   Following in the footsteps of Russian Yuri Gagarin in April 1961, American astronaut John Glenn becomes only the second human in history to orbit the Earth. In just under 5 hours he orbits the Earth three times before splashing down in the Atlantic Ocean near Bermuda.

Feb 21st   The two greatest ballet dancers of the day, Margot Fonteyn and Rudolph Nureyev, dance together for the first time in a Royal Ballet production of *Giselle*. Nureyev had only defected from the Soviet Union the year before.

Mar 2nd   *Theatre 62* is formed by the amalgamation of the West Wickham Dramatic Society and the Actories. The suburban theatre company, located on the outskirts of London, quickly establish themselves as stalwarts of regional theatre.

Mar 5th   The Philips company of The Netherlands releases the first compact audio cassette. They use a high quality 1/8in tape produced by BASF. Recording and playback time is at a rate of 1 7/8 inches per second.

Mar 6th   Due to mounting debts Accrington Stanley football club resign from the football league. Their results from the 1961/2 season are struck from the records.

Mar 15th   The ruling Conservative government is dealt a hammer blow as the Liberal Party takes the seat of Orpington in a surprise by-election victory. Eric Lubbock overturns a 14,760 Conservative majority to win by 7,855 votes.

Mar 18th   The 7th *Eurovision Song Contest* is held at Villa Louvigny in Luxembourg. It is won by France with the song *Un Premier Amour* (A First Love) sung by Isabelle Aubret. The United Kingdom representative Ronnie Carroll, with his song Ring-a-Ding Girl, finishes tied for fourth. Belgium, Spain, Austria and the Netherlands all receive "Nul Points."

Mar 19th   Bob Dylan releases his first album simply titled *Bob Dylan*. The record mostly features reworkings of old blues numbers with only two of the thirteen tracks being new and original songs.

Mar 23rd   Crackwyn Cockspur, a Wire Fox Terrier owned by Mr. Harry L. Gill, wins best in show at the London dog show *Crufts*.

Mar 26th   British Railways chairman Dr. Beeching formally opens the new, state-of-the-art Plymouth station. Designed by architects Howard Cavanagh and Ian Campbell, it took a full six years to complete.

Mar 29th   The Education Act 1962 requires Local Education Authorities to provide grants and pay tuition fees for all students in full-time university education, replacing the former system of state scholarship.

Mar 31st   The Grand National Steeplechase at Aintree is won by 28/1 shot Kilmore, ridden by Fred Winter.

Apr 4th   The A6 murderer, James Hanratty, is hanged at Bedford jail for the murder of scientist Michael Gregsten.

Apr 8th   British nominees have mixed fortunes at the 35th Academy Awards (Oscars) presented by *Ol' Blue Eyes* himself, Frank Sinatra. David Lean takes the Best Director award for *Lawrence of Arabia* while Jack Howells collects the Best Documentary Short Oscar for *Dylan Thomas*. Peter O'Toole, Angela Lansbury and Terrence Stamp, though nominated, all miss out.

Apr 17th   Founded in 1956 by Italian brothers Frank and Aldo Berni, The Berni Inn chain of steakhouses floats on the London Stock Exchange.

Apr 10th   Former Beatle Stuart Sutcliffe dies from a brain haemorrhage in Hamburg.

Apr 20th   Lou Groen, who runs a McDonalds franchise in Cincinnati, introduces the Filet-O-Fish sandwich in reaction to declining meat sales on Friday's.

Apr 28th   On their first season back in the top flight, Ipswich Town win the First Division Championship under the stewardship of manager Alf Ramsey. It looks like he has a bright future in the game.

May 5th   Tottenham Hotspur win back-to-back FA Cups overcoming Burnley 3-1 in the final. Jimmy Greaves is amongst the scorers for the victors.

May 22nd   John Brookes introduces the concept of the modern garden as the "room outside". The multiple, gold medal winning gardener takes the Chelsea Flower Show by storm. The show ends on the 24th with the landscape gardener scooping yet another top award.

May 22nd   In the USA, a bomb explodes in the lavatory of Continental Airlines Flight 11 en route from Chicago to Kansas City, Illinois. All 45 on board are killed. Suspicion falls on passenger William G Doty, who the FBI discovers has taken out extra life insurance to provide for his wife and daughter. He has also recently purchased six sticks of dynamite for two dollars.

May 25ᵗʰ The Queen's Birthday Honours are published in the London Gazette. There is a Damehood for opera singer Eva Turner whilst the Principal Choreographer at the Royal Ballet, Fredrick Ashton, receives a Knighthood.

May 25ᵗʰ The Cathedral Church of St Michael, informally known as Coventry Cathedral, is consecrated. The original structure had been destroyed by the German bombing of Coventry in WWII.

May 31ˢᵗ At around midnight Nazi Adolph Eichmann is hanged in Jerusalem. He was captured and put on trial the previous year for crimes against the Jewish people. It is the only time the death sentence has been carried out in Israel.

Jun 6ᵗʰ The Beatles play their first session at Abbey Road Studios, London.

Jun 8ᵗʰ Something had to give. Marilyn Monroe is fired by 20ᵗʰ Century Fox for her frequent absences during the filming of *Something's Got to Give*.

Jun 12ᵗʰ Guards at Alcatraz Prison in San Francisco Bay check in on three inmates only to find that there are carefully made dummies in their beds. The men are never to be seen again. Did they escape or did they perish in the dangerous waters of the bay?

Jun 13ᵗʰ Lee Harvey Oswald arrives back in the USA on-board the Dutch ocean liner SS Maasdam after spending two years in Russia.

Jun 16ᵗʰ Geoffrey Boycott makes his debut for Yorkshire Cricket Club.

Jun 17ᵗʰ Brazil beat Czechoslovakia 3-1 in the football World Cup Final in Santiago, Chile. Pele, who was injured during the second round of matches, has to watch from the sidelines. Brazil are only the second team to retain the trophy after Italy (1938).

Jul 1ˢᵗ Burundi and Rwanda both gain independence from their European colonisers, Belgium.

Jul 5th   Algeria gains independence from France bringing to a close a brutal conflict which has left over 1 million dead. 900,000 people flee the country as they fear reprisals by the new government.

Jul 7th   Manchester United pay a record transfer fee of £115,000 to secure the services of Denis Law from the Italian team Torino.

Jul 7th   In the world of tennis, Rod Laver defeats fellow Australian Martin Mulligan 6-2, 6-2, 6-1 to lift the Wimbledon title for the second time.

Jul 9th   American Pop Artist Andy Warhol displays his Campbell's Soup Cans for the first time in Los Angeles, California.

Jul 12th   The Rolling Stones play their first gig at the Marquee Jazz Club in London's Oxford Street.

Jul 12th   Telstar 1 transmits the first live television pictures across the Atlantic by satellite. Whilst the images are fuzzy, this clearly marks a great technological leap forward.

Jul 13th   UK Prime Minister Harold Macmillan sacks seven members of his cabinet in a bid to address the growing unpopularity of his government, in what is reported as "The Night of the Long Knives".

Jul 13th   Arnold Palmer wins the Open Tournament held at the Troon Golf Club in Scotland. He leads from the second round onwards and wins by a comfortable six shots from Australian Kel Nagle.

Jul 14th   David Hockney, who is in his final year at the Royal College of Art in London, creates a multi-layered self-portrait in etching and aquatint on paper.

Jul 19th   Frenchman José Meiffret becomes the first cyclist to exceed 200km/h. He sets a world motor-paced speed record of 204km/h (127mph) riding behind a Mercedes-Benz 300SL on a German Autobahn.

Jul 20th   The world's first scheduled passenger hovercraft service is introduced between Rhyl and Wallasey, linking North Wales with Merseyside.

Jul 21ˢᵗ   After a recital of the *National Anthem*, the Proms at London's Royal Albert Hall opens with Benjamin Britten's *The Young Person's Guide to the Orchestra* and features Felix Mendelssohn's interpretation of Shakespeare's *A Midsummer Night's Dream*.

Aug 2ⁿᵈ   Robert Allen Zimmerman legally changes his name to Bob Dylan. He had considered the spelling Dillon before reading the poetry of Welsh bard Dylan Thomas.

Aug 4ᵗʰ   Screen icon Marilyn Monroe dies of a suspected barbiturate overdose. Her body is discovered the next day at her home in Los Angeles, California.

Aug 6ᵗʰ   After more than 300 years Jamaica gains independence from Britain. The Union Jack is ceremonially lowered and replaced by the Jamaican flag throughout the country. Princess Margaret is on hand to open the first session of the island's Parliament on behalf of the Queen, who remains Head of State.

Aug 17ᵗʰ   18-year-old bricklayer Peter Fechter becomes the 27ᵗʰ person to be killed by East German border guards as he tries to cross into West Berlin.

Aug 23ʳᵈ   John Lennon marries Cynthia Powell in a quiet registry office ceremony at Mount Pleasant, Liverpool.

Aug 25ᵗʰ   In Rugby Union, the British Lions under the captaincy of Scotland's Arthur Smith finish an unsuccessful tour of South Africa by being thrashed 34-14 by the host nation in Bloemfontein. They lose the series 3-0.

Sep 2ⁿᵈ   Caught in the middle of a fierce typhoon the British tug SS Kowloondocks sinks in Victoria Harbour, Hong Kong. All 30 on-board are lost at sea.

Sep 6ᵗʰ   Archaeologist Peter Marsden uncovers wooden ships dating back to the second century AD on the banks of the Thames near Blackfriars.

Sep 14ᵗʰ   Actress Janet Leigh (35) divorces actor Tony Curtis (37) after 10 years of marriage.

Sep 15th The Last Night of the Proms is a particularly patriotic affair. It features Elgar's *Pomp and Circumstance March No. 1 in D major*, *Land of Hope and Glory*, Thomas Arne's *Rule Britannia* and Hubert Parry's *Jerusalem*.

Sep 19th Atlantic College enrols students for the first time at St Donat's Castle, west of Cardiff, marking the beginning of the United World College movement.

Sep 21st New Musical Express publishes an article about two 13-year-old schoolgirls releasing a record on the Decca label and adds that "A Liverpool group, The Beatles, have recorded a song *Love Me Do* for Parlophone Records.

Sep 25th The last steam locomotive train to be built in Scotland is shipped from the yard of Andrew Barclay and Sons of Kilmarnock to a customer in Sumatra, Indonesia.

Oct 4th Boys adventure comic *Valiant* sees its first edition. It features Billy Bunter, Sexton Blake and the Steel Claw.

Oct 5th The Beatles release their debut single *Love Me Do*. It peaks at number 17 in the charts.

Oct 15th US Air Force pilot Richard Heyser flies a spy plane over Cuba and takes photographs of Russian medium-range missiles.

Oct 18th Francis Crick (UK), James Watson (US) and Maurice Wilkins (NZ) are awarded the Nobel Prize in Medicine for their work in mapping out the structure of DNA. Rosalind Franklin, who was equally important in the project, goes unrecognised as she died four years previously. Nobel prizes cannot be awarded posthumously.

Oct 20th Chinese forces launch a surprise attack on India. 80,000 Chinese troops attack a force of 20,000 Indians who are defending the Himalayan border region.

Oct 21st The American Folk Blues Festival, touring Europe, plays its only British gig at The Free Trade Hall, Manchester. The audience includes Mick Jagger, Keith Richards, Jimmy Page, Paul Jones and John Mayall.

Oct 26th   Concerned that the Russians will not remove their missiles from Cuba, America draws up plans to invade and seize the missiles. Doing this will most likely result in war, probably nuclear.

Oct 27th   Russian leader Khrushchev says that he will remove the missiles from Cuba if President Kennedy promises not to invade. Kennedy agrees to the proposal. The world goes to bed waiting to see if Khrushchev will accept the arrangement.

Oct 28th   Khrushchev delivers a speech on Radio Moscow and says that he has agreed to Kennedy's arrangement. The missiles will be removed, Cuba will not be invaded and the Cuban Missile Crisis comes to an end. The world breathes a collective sigh of relief.

Nov 7th   Nelson Mandela is sentenced to five years in prison for incitement and leaving the country illegally. He begins serving his sentence at Pretoria Local Prison and is assigned the prisoner number 19476/62.

Nov 14th   Postage stamps are issued in Britain to mark National Productivity Year, an initiative which has cross-party support. The stamps are designed by David Gentleman; each bearing a larger than usual image of the Queen alongside a dynamic design.

Nov 21st   China declares a ceasefire, bringing the Sino-Indian War to an end. In a month of battle, fighting has been fierce with losses heavy on both sides.

Nov 24th   Satire is reborn. *That Was the Week That Was* debuts on British television. David Frost and his team poke fun at the rich and powerful. The show becomes an instant success.

Nov 29th   Britain and France sign a deal to develop Concorde, the world's first supersonic passenger aeroplane.

Nov 29th   West London slum landlord, racketeer and playboy, Peter Rachman dies. Few mourn his passing.

Dec 1st   *Wizard of Oz* author L. Frank Baum's short story *The Tiger's Eye* is published for the first time, 60 years after it was written and over 40 years after the writer's death.

Dec 2nd   A severe smog descended on London lasting for four days. Reminiscent of the deadly smog 10 years earlier, this toxic soup of factory and domestic pollutants kills 106 people; all with pre-existing heart and lung problems.

Dec 6th   The Manson family leave the Isle of Stroma, just north of John O'Groats, Scotland, leaving the island devoid of human inhabitants for the first time in more than a thousand years.

Dec 10th   David Lean's epic film *Lawrence of Arabia,* starring Peter O'Toole, has its worldwide première in London attended by Queen Elizabeth II.

Dec 22nd   An area of high pressure settles over Sweden drawing bitterly cold easterly winds from Russia to the South of England.

Dec 22nd   *Telstar* by The Tornadoes reaches No.1 in the USA; a first for a British band.

Dec 25th   The Queen's Christmas message is broadcast. In it she addresses what Prime Minister Harold Macmillan had earlier broadly called the "Winds of Change." In part of her speech, she states that "There is something wonderful in the way these old familiar warmhearted words of the traditional Christmas message never seem to grow stale. Surely it is because the family festival is like a firm landmark in the stormy seas of modern life.

    Year by year, our families change and grow up. So does our Commonwealth family. This year Jamaica, Trinidad and Tobago and Uganda have joined the circle as full members and we wish them all good fortune."

Dec 26th   An Express train travelling from Liverpool Lime Street to Birmingham New Street collides with a stationary Glasgow to London train in dreadful winter conditions. The crash leaves 18 people dead and 34 seriously injured.

Dec 29th   Blizzards sweep across Southwest England and South Wales causing snowdrifts of up to 20ft (6.1m).

 ### Peter Hugh Dennis aka Hugh Dennis
born on 13th February 1962 in Kettering, Northamptonshire, UK

While studying geography at Cambridge, Dennis' nickname was "desk." His ability to sit and study served him well as he got a first class degree. It didn't however stop him pursuing his other passion, comedy. Dennis was active in the famous and influential Cambridge University Footlights where he formed a partnership with Steve Punt. The two would become leading figures in British satire from the mid-eighties onwards. After graduating he worked for Unilever meaning comedy had to take a back seat. Dennis got his big break when his talent for mimicry got him a role on *Spitting Image* in 1989. He then went on to co-create *The Mary Whitehouse Experience* with David Baddiel, Rob Newman and Steve Punt. Topical satire has always been close to Dennis' heart; he had a regular fixture on the panel show *Mock the Week* since it first aired in 2005 until 2022. His main comedy platform is as co-presenter of Radio 4's *The Now Show*, an irreverent look at the weekly news. Dennis is also a dab hand at situation comedy, most famously playing the father in BBC's *Outnumbered* where he picked up the award for Best TV Comedy Actor at the British Comedy Awards in 2011. He also stars as Lee Mack's neighbour in *Not Going Out*.

Dennis has stated that whilst at Cambridge he was approached by the security service MI5. After attending an initial interview, he decided not to pursue the matter after being told that the job involved "doing people over". He did however briefly feature in the 2021 Bond film *No Time To Die* as a scientist in an MI6 laboratory.

 ### John Francis Bongiovi Jr. aka Jon Bon Jovi
born on 2nd March 1962 in Perth Amboy, New Jersey, USA

There must have been something they put in the fertiliser in the Garden State, for New Jersey has produced some of America's greatest musical artists. Springsteen, Sinatra, Paul Simon, Whitney Houston and Frankie Valli were all born there. Added to that list is one of the State's most enigmatic figures, Jon Bon Jovi. He formed his rock band in 1983 calling it simply Bon Jovi. They released their first album in 1984, which spawned a top 40 hit *Runaway*. The next year, *7800° Fahrenheit* was released and became a top seller. In 1986 the band went global with the release of *Slippery When Wet*. When Jon teamed up with songwriter Desmond Child, it took his music to yet another level and together they wrote over 30 songs. Always striving for something new and cutting edge, Bon Jovi embarked on a solo career and his album *Blaze of Glory* was released to great critical acclaim on both sides of the Atlantic. His abundant rock star good looks took him into acting where he played Helen Hunt's ex-husband in *Play it Forward*. He also appeared on the small screen in *Sex in the City* and *Ally McBeal*. Bon Jovi has contributed time and funds to many charitable works. He made a huge donation to build homes in Philadelphia. This project was called Habitat for Humanity. He was a founding ambassador for the program and donated $1 million dollars to get it started.

On his success Jon Bon Jovi stated "There is not a platinum record hanging up in my house.....they are all in the garage in bubble wrap."

Sir Steven Geoffrey Redgrave CBE DL
born on 23rd March 1962 in Marlow, Buckinghamshire, UK

Redgrave is without doubt Britain's greatest ever Olympian. It is not just the fact that he won five gold medals in successive Olympic Games, it is that his fourth gold in the Atlanta games of 1996 represented Team GB's only gold medal. Redgrave's achievements came largely when funding for his sport was poor compared to today. Away from the Olympics, he was part of teams that won nine World Championship gold medals.

He also competed at the Henley Royal Regatta for more than two decades, winning fifteen cups and goblets. Whilst he was more accustomed to racing in coxless pairs and fours, his greatest individual achievement was in winning the Wingfield Skulls five years in succession. The event is for single skullers and is raced on the Thames over the Oxford and Cambridge Boat Race course between Putney and Mortlake. In 2002 his fifth Olympic gold was voted the greatest British sporting achievement by Channel 4 Viewers. In 2006 Redgrave ran the London Marathon raising £1.8m for charity. Not bad for a working class lad from Buckinghamshire who has suffered from diabetes.

After his victory in Atlanta in 1996, Redgrave said that "If anyone sees me go near a boat you've my permission to shoot me." Thankfully no one did as he returned to win another gold four years later.

Richard Keith Robert Coles FRSA FKC
born on 26th March 1962 in Northampton, UK

To say that Coles has had a rich and varied career is truly an understatement. Coles studied Theology at King's College London before turning to music and linking up with Jimmy Somerville, first in Bronski Beat and then the Communards. Three top ten hits followed including their biggest *Don't Leave Me This Way*. The pair were not only high on success but also on drugs. Coles decided that their debauched lifestyle was not for him and returned to religion. He gained entry to the College of the Resurrection to train as a priest. He was ordained in 2005 and served as curate in Lincolnshire and London before taking up the post of vicar at St. Mary the Virgin in Finedon, Northamptonshire. Coles' rich voice and confident demeanour made him not only a natural for the pulpit, but also for radio. He took over the reins at Radio 4's *Saturday Live* in 2011 gracing the airways with his laid back manner. On 1st November 2012 All Saints' Day, Darton, Longman and Todd published Coles' book, *Lives of the Improbable Saints*, illustrated by Ted Harrison. The book was a précis of the life stories of nearly 200 lesser-known saints. The following year, Volume two *Legends of the Improbable Saints* was published. In 2022 he retired as the vicar of Finedon on Low Sunday, the Sunday after Easter. He explained "I will still be a priest, I will always be a priest, and I will minister where I am able."

Coles was the inspiration for the character Adam Smallbone in the BBC sitcom Rev and was also an advisor to the show.

 ### Phillip Bryan Schofield
born on 1st April 1962 in Oldham, Lancashire, UK

Schofield's first foray into the media business came when he was 15 at Hospital Radio Plymouth. He found that not only did he have a passion for the work, he also had great natural ability. For the next couple of years he pestered the BBC for a job. At age 17 he was offered the role of bookings clerk and general dogsbody for BBC Radio at Broadcasting House in London. Aged 19 he moved with his parents to New Zealand where he landed a job as presenter on the youth music programme *Shazam!*. In 1985 he returned to Britain as a seasoned professional and became the face of children's television presenting from *The Broom Cupboard* alongside mischievous puppet Gordon the Gopher. Two years later he would become the face of Saturday mornings presenting *Going Live* with Sarah Greene. He also hosted the *Smash Hits Poll Winners Party*. In the early 1990s he switched to adult-oriented television in *Schofield's Quest*, *Schofield's TV Gold* and *Talking Telephone Numbers*. In 2002 he cemented his position as the face of daytime television when he replaced John Leslie as host of ITV's *This Morning* alongside Fern Britten. Since 2009 he was joined by co-host Holly Willoughby; famous for their legendary laughing fits. Between times he has appeared on stage as *Dr. Doolittle* and Joseph in *Joseph and the Amazing Technicolor Dreamcoat*. He has also hosted *The Cube* game show and *Dancing On Ice*.

Schofield is an avid wine buff. His interest was first kindled when he was given two cases of Burgundy as payment for introducing a compilation video for Jason Donovan.

 ### Evan Harold Davis
born on 8th April 1962 in Malvern, Worcestershire, UK

Evan Davis is one of the most recognisable faces and voices on British TV and radio. He studied at St. John's College Oxford (1981 to 1984) and at the Kennedy School of Government at Harvard University (1986 to 1988). After working as an economist at the London Business School, Davis joined the BBC in 1993. Evan Davis is the presenter of *PM*, the news and current affairs programme that airs weekdays and Saturdays on Radio 4. Before taking up that role in November 2018, he was the main presenter of BBC2's *Newsnight* (from 2014). Before this he was a presenter of the *Today* programme on BBC Radio 4 (2008–2014). He is also well-known as the presenter of the BBC2 business reality show *Dragons' Den*. And on Radio 4, he hosts a weekly business discussion programme *The Bottom Line*. He has made several BBC documentaries, including the influential two-part BBC2 series *Mind the Gap* (2014) which explored the economic disparities between London and the regions. In 2011 he presented *Made in Britain*, a three-part BBC2 series with an accompanying book on how the country pays its way in the world. In 2011, Evan was also one of a number of journalists involved in a BBC1 Panorama special called *Breaking into Britain*, a moving account of the journeys migrants take to get into Europe and the UK.

In spite of it being so pivotal to much of his life, Davis stated "I actually profoundly think the world's a better place when economics is fairly boring... The more boring the better."

 ## Michelle Danielle Collins
born on 28th May 1962 in Hackney, London, UK

Collins' career path into acting was initially orthodox before taking an unexpected musical turn. From the age of 14 she trained at the Royal Court and the Cockpit Youth Theatre landing a role in Mikhail Bulgakov's *The Crimson Island*. Her career took a sharp turn when she appeared in the 1978 video for the Squeeze song *Cool For Cats*. This led to a year and a half touring with the band performing with other artists including Kid Creole and Level 42. When Squeeze broke up in 1982, Michelle returned to acting. She had minor parts in *The Bill*, the sitcom *Running Wild* and *Bergerac*. It was while she was performing in the BBC play *Pressures* in 1988 she was spotted by *EastEnders* producer Julia Smith who asked her to audition for the role of Cindy Williams. Initially given the role for 11 episodes her character drew the attention of local Lotharios as well as adulation from the viewing public. When her role was made permanent, her character somehow found herself married to perennial small businessman Ian Beale. It was a role she played with great gusto, pitched somewhere between Cruella de Vil and Fanny Hill. She left *EastEnders* after ten successful years. Controversy followed when she joined *Coronation Street* in 2011 as Stella Price, landlady of the Rover's Return. Public criticism of her accent along with her perceived lack of storylines saw her quit in 2014. She published her autobiography, *This is Me*, in 2014.

Collins recommended Spandau Ballet bassist Martin Kemp for the role of Steve Owen in EastEnders. He then followed a similar path to her own from music to soap opera.

 ## Eamonn Roderique Walker
born on 12th June 1962 in London, UK

Walker has stated that he was inspired to be an actor after watching Sidney Poitier in *In the Heat of the Night*. However his first major TV role was when he was cast a gay home help in *In Sickness and in Health*. The series featured bigoted Alf Garnett and the jokes "flowed" from their relationship. A year in ITV's *The Bill* followed along with appearances in *Birds of a Feather*, *One Foot in the Grave* and *Bergerac*. None of these were really the roles Walker craved, so he did what many black British actors of his generation did. He not only went to America, he turned himself into an American.

Hollywood was as hungry for him as he was for Hollywood with major roles swiftly following his arrival. From 1997 to 2003 he had a major role in HBO's *Oz* playing a devout Muslim in a fictional maximum security prison. Film roles followed including playing alongside Bruce Willis and Samuel L. Jackson in the 2000 film *Unbreakable*. In 2003 he starred alongside Bruce Willis in the film *Tears of the Sun* and in 2005 he co-starred with Nicholas Cage in crime thriller *Lord of War*. On Broadway he has performed as Mark Anthony in *Julius Caesar* alongside Denzel Washington whilst he became the first black actor to play Othello at the Globe Theatre in London. Walker lives in the USA with his wife Sandra and their three children.

Walker began his career as a dancer but when injury forced him to give it up he turned to acting.

Thomas Cruise Mapother IV aka Tom Cruise
born on 3rd July 1962 in Syracuse, New York, USA

After leaving the seminary where he was training to be a priest, Cruise ditched his surname and embarked on a career in acting under the altogether more catchy name, Tom Cruise. His first role was that of Billy in 1981's *Endless Love*, a film notable for its soundtrack and little else. It was clear though that Cruise's good looks and winning smile would see him go a long way in the business. He landed his first starring role in *Risky Business* (1983), before he played Maverick in *Top Gun* (1986) which cemented his position as Hollywood royalty. Before the decade was out he starred in *The Color of Money*, *Rain Man* and *Born on the Fourth of July*. In the 1990s his hits included *A Few Good Men*, *The Firm* and *Jerry Maguire*. It is remarkable for such a famous actor that he has never won an Oscar; his last nomination for *Magnolia* coming over twenty years ago. But Cruise has never been about critical acclaim. Many of his movies were only given three star ratings by critics but the box office told a different story. He became the first actor to star in five consecutive films that grossed over $100m dollars in the US. More recently Cruise has produced and starred in the *Mission: Impossible* and *Jack Reacher* franchises and in 2022 he reprised the role of Maverick in an updated version of *Top Gun*. Cruise has been married 3 times and has 3 children. He is also famously an advocate for the Church of Scientology.

Cruise insists on performing many of his own stunts, including climbing the exterior of the half-mile-high Burj Khalifa in Dubai, hanging from the outside of a plane during take-off and a high speed helicopter chase, all during the filming of *Mission: Impossible* franchise films.

Neil Anthony Morrissey
born on 4th July 1962 in Stafford, Staffordshire, UK

Neil Morrissey has a rare talent as a comic actor; he can make people laugh whilst seeming to have great fun at the same time. After leaving drama school he had bit parts in police series *Juliet Bravo* and *C.A.T.S Eyes*. In 1987 he landed his first major role when he played sidekick Rocky Cassidy to Michael Elphick's fireman-cum-private detective, *Boon*. His boyish good looks and abundant charm made him an instant hit. He stayed with the hit series for 74 episodes. When, in 1992, Harry Enfield decided to leave the series *Men Behaving Badly*, Morrissey was a natural pick to enter as Martin Clunes' partner-in-crime. His on screen/off screen romance with co-star Leslie Ash filled the pages of the gossip columns, as well as allowing them to cash in by making adverts. In 2009 Morrissey took a break from acting to run a pub in Yorkshire. Refreshed, he returned to acting, this time taking more serious parts in dramas such as *Line of Duty* and *The Night Manager*. Children will recognise him as the voice behind *Bob the Builder*. Since 2004 Morrissey has invested in a number of properties including pubs and hotels since 2004. His love of Dylan Thomas led him buy up a number of properties in the village Laugharne in Wales where Thomas lived out his final days. He now owns a chains of pubs in Staffordshire. Morrissey has had a number of high-profile relationships including Amanda Holden and Rachel Weisz.

He grew up in care and, desperate for a more stable environment, placed an advert for foster parents on his school noticeboard. The advert was successful.

 Tracy Edwards MBE
born on 5th September 1962 in Reading, Berkshire, UK

At the age of fifteen Edwards was expelled from school with no qualifications, so she decided to travel the world. She began working on luxury yachts in Greece at the age of seventeen. It is there that she first learned how to sail. Tracy took part in her first Whitbread Round the World Race as cook aboard 'Atlantic Privateer' in 1985/6, becoming the first woman to race around the world on a Maxi class yacht. Upon completion, she decided to enter the first all-female crew in the 1989/90 Whitbread race. 'Maiden' crossed the start line on 2nd September 1989 and sailed into the history books. Edwards and her crew went on to win two of the legs and came second in class overall, the best result for a British boat since 1977 and the best result for an all-female crew ever. Tracy was awarded the MBE and became the first woman in its 34 year history to win the Yachtsman of the Year Award. In 2007 and 2008 Tracy worked for CEOP (Child Exploitation and Online Protection) as a Project Manager for their International Youth Advisory Conference. Working with the UN she assisted in the creation of a 2009 resolution regarding child safety to the UNCRC. At the end of her contract Tracy enrolled at Roehampton University taking a degree in Psychology, graduating with an upper second.

In 2014 Edwards discovered that the yacht 'Maiden' lay stricken and in poor condition in a harbour in the Indian Ocean. With the help of Princess Haya of Jordan, the boat was restored and in 2018 it departed from Southampton with an all-female crew on board.

 Jameel Sadik "Jim" Al-Khalili CBE FRS FInstP
born on 20th September 1962 in Baghdad, Iraq

Al-Khalili is a theoretical physicist, author, respected BBC presenter and frequent commentator about science in the British media. He is a great teacher who he can impart what he knows to people at every level, be they the person in the street or a group of PHD students. That Al-Khalili, who gets his name from his Iraqi father, should have become a scientist was almost written in the stars. He shares his name with a great Islamic astronomer who compiled extensive tables for timekeeping by the Sun in the 14th Century. His academic career has been stellar. He became a Fellow of the Institute of Physics in 2000, won the Michael Faraday Prize for communication in 2007 and has received the Institute's Public Awareness of Physics Award. Among other roles he is an external examiner for the Open University and sits on the advisory committee for the Cheltenham Science Festival. It seems at times that he must have found a way of expanding time itself. He has numerous publications to his name, both in popular and hard science. He has hosted many documentaries including Channel 4's *The Riddle of Einstein's Brain*, featured on many radio broadcasts including *The Life Scientific* on BBC Radio 4 and hosts a YouTube channel where he interviews scientists and spiritual leaders. All this has taken place while he still holds down a professorship at the University of Surrey.

Al-Khalili was President of Humanist UK from 2013-2016. He has reflected that as the son of a Protestant Christian mother and a Shia Muslim father he nevertheless ended up without a religious bone in his body,

🎵 Tracey Anne Thorn
born on 26th September 1962 in Brookmans Park, Herts, UK

Thorn is best known for being one half of the musical duo Everything But The Girl (the other half being her husband, Ben Watt). She met Watt whilst studying at university in Hull. Initially they pursued separate musical careers signing for Cherry Red Records as solo artists until they formed their band in 1982. Success, however, was not instantaneous. Between 1983 and 1988 they produced ten singles with only one top-thirty hit. During this time Thorn also contributed guest vocals on songs for other bands including The Style Council and Lloyd Cole and the Commotions. For Everything But The Girl album sales were better with 1985's *Love Not Money* reaching number 10 in the UK charts. The duo's biggest chart success came in 1995 when DJ Todd Terry remixed a song from their album *Amplified Heart. Missing* became a global hit, including in the US where it peaked at number 2 in the Billboard Hot 100.

Thorn also had a successful collaboration with Massive Attack in the 1990s including the critically acclaimed track *Protection*. When Everything But The Girl stopped recording in 1999, Thorn remained active in the music industry. She has also written 4 memoirs including the critically acclaimed *Bedsit Disco Queen, How I Grew Up and Tried to be a Pop Star.* In 2014 she began a regular fortnightly column, 'Off The Record', for the British political and cultural magazine New Statesman.

Due to social anxiety and the demands of family life, Thorn has never performed live.

🎬 Alicia Christian "Jodie" Foster
born on 19th November 1962 in Los Angeles, California, USA

Jodie Foster began her career making TV commercials aged just three. Her first full acting role came aged six, in the TV drama series *Mayberry RFD*. In 1975 she was offered the role of child prostitute Iris Steensma in *Taxi Driver* alongside Robert De Niro. That such a demanding role was given to a thirteen-year-old is testament to Foster's maturity and acting ability. She also thanked De Niro for his emotional support. In 1980 she graduated top of her class from the College Lycée Français and went on to study English Literature at Yale. On 30th March 1981, John Hinkley attempted to assassinate President Ronald Reagan. It later transpired that Hinkley had become obsessed with the film *Taxi Driver* (which featured an attempt on a President's life) and Jodie Foster in particular. Despite the fact that she never took acting lessons, she joined a select band of actors who won two Oscars before reaching the age of 30. Her first was for her role as Sarah Tobias in *The Accused* (1988) and her second was for her performance as Clarice Starling in *The Silence of the Lambs* (1991). In 1992 she set up her own production company, Egg Pictures. Successful productions included *Nell, Sommersby* and *Contact.* In the early 2000s she suffered a setback when Egg Pictures closed down. She subsequently starred in a number of successful films including *Panic Room, Flightplan* and *Inside Man.* Since the 2010s she has focussed her talents on directing films and TV series alongside her acting.

Foster often dubs her own character's voice for French versions of her films as she is fluent.

 ## Ralph Nathaniel Twisleton-Wykeham-Fiennes
born on 22nd December 1962 in Ipswich, Suffolk, UK

Fiennes first came to prominence as a theatre actor with the Royal National Theatre. Throughout a distinguished career, his canon of theatrical performances has earned him much critical acclaim. He has played Hamlet on Broadway for which he won a Tony Award, also Romeo, Richard II and Richard III to name but four. It is his work on film that has brought him to the wider public's attention. His big break came when his rugged good looks saw him cast as Heathcliff in Peter Kominsky's *Wuthering Heights*. He then caught the eye of Stephen Spielberg who cast him as the Nazi concentration camp Commandant, Amon Göth, in *Schindler's List;* a role in which he earned a BAFTA award.

Robert Redford was the next director to call on the enigmatic actor when he cast him as Charles Van Doren in *Quizshow*, a film about a scandal that rocked American TV. His A-list status was secure. He has also starred in *The English Patient, The Constant Gardener* and *The Grand Budapest Hotel.* Year-on-year he has appeared in successful movies, landing recurring roles as Q in the *Bond* franchise and Lord Voldemort in the *Harry Potter* series.

Fiennes comes from an extremely creative family. His brother Joseph is also an actor, sisters Martha and Sophie are a director and a producer respectively, whilst another brother Magnus is a musician. His third cousin once-removed is the acclaimed explorer Sir Ranulph Fiennes.

 # Other Notable Births

 Jim Carrey
17th January 1962
Actor | Comedian

 Axl Rose
6th February 1962
Singer | Songwriter

 Eddie Izzard
7th February 1962
Comedian | Actor

 Vanessa Feltz
21st February 1962
Broadcaster | Journalist

 John Hannah
23rd April 1962
Actor

 Stuart Pearce
24th April 1962
Footballer | Manager

 Jimmy White
2nd June 1962
Snooker Player

 Paula Abdul
19th June 1962
Singer | Actress

 Phill Jupitus
25th June 1962
Comedian | Actor

 Michael Ball
27th June 1962
Singer | Broadcaster

 Amanda Donohoe
29th June 1962
Actress

 Shaun Ryder
23rd August 1962
Singer | Songwriter

 Steve Irwin
4th September 1962
Wildlife Expert

 John Fashanu
18th September 1962
Footballer | Presenter

 Demi Moore
11th November 1962
Actress

 ### Salvatore Luciana aka Charles "Lucky" Luciano
died aged 64 on 26th January 1962 in Naples, Italy

When Luciana's family brought him to America aged just eight, he saw it as a land of opportunity. Sadly for America that opportunity involved mainly crime. As a young man he ran illicit gambling, prostitution and bootlegging operations. "Lucky" acquired his nickname when he survived a murder attempt in 1929. He never spoke of those who were responsible, but brutal retribution was meted out. He ordered a hit on the Mafia boss, Joe Masseria, which cleared his path to be head of the mob. The authorities caught up with "Lucky" in 1935 when he was imprisoned. Incarceration did not stop Lucania's control where he continued to run his organisation from behind bars. Ever the player, World War II provided "Lucky" opportunity. His mobsters controlled the port unions. Fearing crippling strikes, the authorities commuted his sentence in 1946. He initially fled to Cuba but then returned to Italy where he eventually died of a heart attack.

 ### Victoria Mary (Vita) Sackville-West, Lady Nicholson CH
died aged 70 on 2nd June 1962 at Sissinghurst Castle, Kent, UK

As a novelist, poet and gardener Victoria grew up in her family's ancestral estate, Knole, in Kent. During her life she wrote a dozen collections of poetry including the 1946 publication *The Garden,* which combined her two greatest passions of horticulture and writing. She is also known for her personal and literary connections to members of the Bloomsbury Group of writers, including Virginia Woolf who described her as the inspiration for the main character in her 1928 novel *Orlando.* Though married, West was thought to have had many lovers including Virginia Woolf herself. West's enduring legacy are the beautifully constructed gardens at Sissinghurst which she created with her husband. In 1948 she became a founder member of the National Trust's garden committee and was awarded the Veitch Memorial medal by the Royal Horticultural Society. It is fitting that the beautiful garden at Sissinghurst is now managed by the National Trust.

 ### Marilyn Monroe (born Norma Jean Mortenson)
died aged 36 on 4th August 1962 in Los Angeles, California, USA

From her first credited role in *Dangerous Year* (1947), where she played a waitress, to her last finished film, *The Misfits* (1961), Monroe stole every scene she appeared in. Her filmography tells the story of her meteoric rise and catastrophic decline. Between 1951 and 1953 she appeared in over a dozen films; by the early 1960s that number had dwindled to one a year. Alcohol and drug abuse, as well as three failed marriages, had begun to take their toll. She was the most exploited celebrity of the twentieth century. Hugh Hefner used her body to launch Playboy magazine, Andy Warhol used her face to create art and advertisers used her image to sell everything from soap to cigarettes. By the late 1950s Monroe's behaviour was becoming ever more erratic. On August 4th 1962, alone on her bed in her apartment at 12305 Helena Drive, Los Angeles, she took her own life. The flame that had shone so brightly was extinguished all too soon.

 ## Patrick Hamilton
died aged 58 on 23rd September 1962 in Sheringham, Norfolk, UK

Hamilton's father was a writer, fantasist and an alcoholic who believed himself to be the rightful heir to the Scottish throne. His financial ineptitude led his family from comfortable surroundings near Brighton to the less salubrious boarding houses of West London. This gave Patrick an affinity for the poor and powerless with many critics comparing his writing favourably to that of Charles Dickens. His first writing success was the stage play *Rope*, later adapted for cinema by Alfred Hitchcock. His most enduring legacy is the play *Gas Light*, which spawned two film versions; one starring Ingrid Bergman. It centres around coercive control in a marriage and has given the English language the word gaslighting. *Hangover Square* is considered his finest work and stands as one of the greatest novels set in London. Hamilton was a far better writer than his father, but sadly also a more self-destructive alcoholic. He died of cirrhosis of the liver aged just 58.

Niels Henrick David Bohr
died aged 77 on 18th November 1962 in Copenhagen, Denmark

Bohr was born into a family steeped in science. As a young man he was a difficult student as he knew far more than most of his teachers and also believed that a lot of scientific thinking of the time was wrong. He went on to gain a masters and a doctorate from the University of Copenhagen before coming to Cambridge to study. Again he was not the happiest of students. When Bohr met Ernest Rutherford he had finally encountered a teacher who he respected. In 1922 Bohr was awarded the Nobel Prize in Physics for "his services in the investigation of the structure of atoms and of the radiation emanating from them." Bohr not only shaped the history of the twentieth century, his life was also greatly affected by it. When the Nazis invaded Denmark, his Jewish heritage meant his life was in danger. He fled by boat to Sweden and then America, to work on the Manhattan Project, which created the first Atomic Bomb.

Charles Laughton
died aged 63 on 15th December 1962 in Hollywood, California, USA

Charles Laughton was probably the greatest character actor Britain has ever produced, perhaps only rivalled by Sir Alec Guinness. Having survived a gas attack on the Western Front during the First World War, Laughton embarked on a career in acting. He knew that he would never play the romantic lead and disparagingly described his face as being like the "behind of an elephant." But Laughton's face would be his fortune. He could with ease express scorn, exude menace and melt hearts. His rich voice was almost hypnotising. Laughton's rotund figure was well suited to the role of the King in 1933's *The Private Life of Henry VIII*. Perhaps his most famous role, which also highlighted his lack of vanity, was as Quasimodo in *The Hunchback of Notre Dame* in 1939. In 1956 Laughton stood in for Ed Sullivan and was the first person to introduce Elvis Presley to a US TV audience.

The Coins We Used

9 years before decimalisation, the United Kingdom used the system of **pounds**, **shillings** and **pence**, commonly represented using the symbols **£sd**. The **£** symbol evolved over many years from the letter **L** which derives from the Latin word *libra*, meaning a pound of money. Although **s** is the first letter of the word shilling, the use of the letter derives from the Latin word *solidus*, which means coin. The curious use of the letter **d** for pennies also has a Latin origin from the word *denarius*, meaning containing ten.

Unlike the decimal system based on multiples of 10, the pre-decimal system was based on multiples of 12. There were 12 pennies to a shilling and 240 pennies to a pound. This meant there were 20 shillings to the pound. In 1962 there were 8 coins in circulation with evocative names that still permeate our language today. Note: The farthing (¼ d) ceased to be legal tender a year earlier in 1961.

	Halfpenny ½ d *In use to 1969*	Commonly known as the *ha'penny* it is was the only word in the English language with a silent 'f'. Since 1937 the coin featured Sir Francis Drake's ship The Golden Hind. The popular pub game *Shove Ha'penny* features 5 halfpennies.
	Penny 1d *In use to 1971*	Before 1860 the penny was a large copper coin. This is why bicycles with a large front wheel were nicknamed Penny Farthings. Popular expressions using the penny include *ten a penny* and *a penny for your thoughts*.
	Threepence 3d *In use to 1971*	These 12-sided coins were commonly known as *thruppence* or *thrupenny bits*. The silver versions known as *joeys* were often hidden in Christmas puddings making an exciting find for the lucky children who discovered them.
	Sixpence 6d *In use to 1980*	These silver coins reputedly brought good luck. Sixpences were placed in bride's shoes as a wedding gesture. Known as benders, they could easily be bent. *Going on a bender* derived from drinking all day in pubs with sixpence.
	Shilling 1/- *In use to 1990*	First minted in the reign of Henry VII as a testoon, the shilling was latterly commonly known as a bob. *Taking the king's shilling* meant enrolling in the army whilst *A few bob short of a pound* describes someone a bit dim.
	Florin 2/- *In use to 1992*	The florin was Britain's first decimal coin in response to calls in the mid 19th Century for decimal coinage to be introduced. As 2 *bob* the florin was worth 1/10th of a pound. After decimalisation in 1971 florins became worth 10 pence.
	Half Crown 2/6 *In use to 1969*	Half crowns were originally struck in gold in the reign of Henry VIII. The first silver half crowns were issued under Edward VI in 1549. Surviving for over 450 years, the half crown was one of the most successful coins of all time.
	Crown 5/- *In use to present day*	The British crown is a heavy silver coin. Rarely spent, crowns are often minted for commemorative purposes. After decimalisation a crown was worth 25p until 1990 when their face value was changed to £5.

The average annual wage in the UK in 1962 was approximately:

£700-£900

The Mark I Ford Cortina was launched in the UK in 1962. Originally to be named the Ford Consul 225, the car was launched as the Consul Cortina until a facelift in 1964 when the Consul name was dropped. The 50hp standard model would go from 0-60 in 22.5 seconds using its 1198 cc, 4 cylinder engine. Base model prices started at:

£590

The price of the average house would be approximately 3-5x the average annual wage. Depending on where you were in the country this meant the price of a typical 1930's 3-bedroom semi-detached house would be in the region of:

£2,500 - £3,000

The Olympia Splendid 33 portable manual typewriter cost:

£23

In 1962 the average cost for a loaf of white bread would have been:

11½d

A gallon of petrol (which is equivalent to 4.5 litres) cost:

4s 11d

Working Overseas

"Ten Pound Poms" en route to Australia on-board SS New Australia

At work on a rubber plantation in Malaysia

The ten pound assisted passage scheme to Australia proved extremely popular, with two clear waves of migration occurring, firstly in the immediate post-war period, and then peaking in the 1960s. These 'Ten Pound Poms', as they became known (82% were English), were mostly from an urban background and were motivated by various factors: to escape post-war austerity, to take advantage of a warmer climate and an outdoor lifestyle, or to fulfil a sense of adventure. Migrants were required to stay for two years, giving up their passports on arrival, able only to return to Britain if they paid back their outward fare in full, in addition to paying for their journey home. At the beginning of the period there was a focus on assisting migrants who had certain skill-sets, such as building tradesmen or nurses, but by the 1960s there was less emphasis placed on these requirements. A preference for married migrants under the age of 51 and for single migrants under 46 remained. Health checks were conducted to ensure applicants suffering from diseases such as tuberculosis were not accepted. Other overseas opportunities for women included working as an au pair, a governess or in teaching and academia. For men there were roles in management in former colonies. One such role was to be found in the rubber plantations of Malaysia which gained independence from Britain in 1957.

Life on a Rubber Plantation: After an interview and upon acceptance, young men would sign up for anywhere between 4 and 7 years. The initial role was as trainee estate manager. Even though it afforded great privilege, it was not without hardship. For many it was their first time away from home comforts and family. They would have to learn how to tap rubber (though this would never be their job), speak Malay and get used to the sweltering heat which necessitated starting work at sunrise. Anyone who couldn't hack it would not only have to fund their own fare home, but in many cases would have to pay the company for their outward journey. This could lead to great financial hardship. If the trainee gained promotion to estate manager, they were afforded a driver and a housekeeper. Although they were masters of all they surveyed, they faced a difficult balancing act. Local Malays were employed as clearers of the jungle with Tamils (originally from Southern India) and Chinese employed as rubber tappers. Keeping everybody happy was a difficult juggling act, compounded by the fact that there was a Chinese communist led insurgency. There were shops on the estate where products from home could be bought, but at great expense. The savvy Brit soon learned to eat as locals did at a fraction of the cost. After work there was always the club, where ex-pats could mingle. Gin in the afternoon, whisky in the evening and settle the bill at the end of the month, was the general rule.

Women's Work

With the exception of the two World Wars when women filled jobs otherwise undertaken by men who were posted overseas, the role of women was little changed for decades. In the early 1960s things were about to change, but only very slowly. In 1962 only 26,000 women gained entry to university with the majority of those hailing from families with an academic background. Even upon graduation things were still unequal. It was only in 1961 that legislation was passed giving women equal pay in the civil service. It wasn't until 1975 that it became illegal to sack a woman for being pregnant. Women could legally be refused service to spend their own money in a pub. This law didn't change until 1982. Women who had

Women mostly occupied administrative roles

gained equal suffrage with men in 1928 increasingly began to demand a right to a proper education, equal pay and affordable childcare. But for most women their work would be in the home. It would start with making breakfast for the whole family, then making sure that the husband was suitably attired for work and that the children were ready for school. Next it was onto the chores: dusting, cleaning, washing, making beds and ironing. Since most houses still didn't have fridges, shopping was a daily task. As supermarkets were a rarity, this required visits to several shops: the butcher, the baker, the greengrocer and mainly on Fridays the fishmonger. The only thing that was delivered to the house in those days was milk. If she found time in the middle of the day, the 60s housewife might have a nice cup of tea with a neighbour. It was then time to collect the children from school and feed them. After that, she would prepare a supper for her husband, which they would eat together. Then it would be time to put the

The daily chores of a 1960s housewife

children to bed, reminding them to brush their teeth and wash their faces. Although it was a man's world, most fathers saw little of their children except at weekends. Women did gain employment but, with some exceptions, this was mainly outside the demands of childcare. Schools reflected this. Girls would learn what were known then as domestic sciences: cooking, sewing and household management. After leaving school some women trained for secretarial roles with the role of school secretary being highly prized as it allowed holidays to coincide with their children's. The 1960s were a time of rapid social and economic change and by the end of the decade attitudes had changed, even though legislation trailed behind.

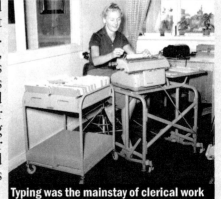
Typing was the mainstay of clerical work

Farming

A typical post-war tractor with open cab

IR8 seeds being packed (credit: IRRI)

Whisky maturing in white oak casks

Although the farm of the 1960s looked very different from the farm of today, increased mechanisation meant that they also looked markedly different from the pre-war farm. Fields were smaller and more work had to be done by hand than today. However, by the end of the decade the greater reliance on machinery not only shaped the crops that were grown (potatoes in particular leant themselves to machine sowing and harvesting), it also saw a 40% decline in the number of farmworkers. Even though the government had brought in controls on pesticides a decade earlier, there was a heavy reliance on chemicals both as pesticides and fertilisers. This was to have serious health implications, not only for farmworkers, but also for the general population. Farms were also dangerous places to work. The tractor, as well as being the most iconic piece of farm machinery, was also the most deadly. An annual average of 43 people were killed from 1957 to 1967 as a result of tractors overturning. This represented over one-third of work-related fatalities in agriculture. It was not until 1967 that legislation was introduced requiring all new tractors to be fitted with safety cabs.

In the 1960s new strains of fruit and vegetables were being developed. The most significant advance came half-way around the world in India. The country was facing impending rice shortages which would inevitably lead to famine. In 1962 Peter Jennings and Henry Beachell, two American plant breeders, successfully cross-bred high yield rice from Indonesia with a dwarf rice from China. The result became known as IR8, and by the end of the decade yields soared and millions of lives were saved. In Scotland a similar, though not as spectacular, thing was happening with the production new strains of barley at the expense of oats and turnips. Although barley has many uses, such as making malted drinks and adding to soups, it was chiefly grown for one thing, the Whisky industry.* Fuelled by rising demand from overseas markets such as America and Japan, the 1960s were boom years for Scottish distillers.

*There has been much debate between whisky connoisseurs, with many claiming that scotch was a much better drink before the 1960s. While this is of course a matter of personal taste, there is no doubt that the rapid expansion of the industry and the way whisky was produced changed the tipple forever. As well as switching to high yield barley, distilling techniques changed as did the way the final product was stored. Previously, Spanish sherry casks were used but by the 1960s these had been replaced by American ex-bourbon white oak casks. This made the final product smoother and more attractive to the American palate. The industry has grown to become Britain's largest food and drink export. This multi-billion pound industry brings in 5 times the revenue of the second biggest, namely chocolate.

The Primary School

In the 1960s there were no state pre-schools or nurseries, so for most children just turning 5 years old, their first day at school was the first time they had been on their own away from home. Many mothers did not work outside the home, so this was also the first time they had been away from the home environment. Consequently, the first day of school was often a very tearful event for both child and parent. Having got over the first pangs of separation, school life soon fell into a predictable routine of learning the times tables, handwriting skills and reading out loud. School milk was part of this routine, and in the summer months it could

An older class busy painting pictures

Harvest festival celebrations

easily turn sour. In post-war Britain school milk, a third of a pint per child, was introduced in schools to supplement the child's diet. In 1971 school milk for the over-sevens was withdrawn by Margaret Thatcher, then Secretary of State for Education – for this she was dubbed 'Thatcher, Thatcher, Milk Snatcher' in the popular press. During the harsh winter of 1962-3, or the big freeze of 1963 as it became known, it was a common sight to see the small crates of milk outside the school gates with the shiny bottle tops standing proud above the bottles on a column of frozen milk. Of course the only way to defrost the school milk was to place it by the radiator, and then the poor children were forced to consume watery, lukewarm milk. And forced they were – "milk is good for your child, you WILL drink it all up!" The School Broadcasting Council for the United Kingdom had been set up in 1947 and the wireless or radio played a great part in the education of school children in the 1960s. *Music and Movement* was one such programme. All over the country in school halls, children could be found leaping and stretching to the commands on the radio. 'Now children we are going to sway like trees in the wind' would be the instruction on the radio so all the children would begin to sway with their arms in the air. There was no 'gym kit' in primary schools so the children just removed their outer clothes and did physical education in their vests, knickers or underpants and bare feet or pumps (usually purchased from F.W. Woolworth). Visits from the school nurse would break up the daily routine. The nit nurse used to make regular visits to check for head lice.

All the children in each class would line up to be examined in turn, their hair being combed carefully with a nit comb to see if there was any infestation. There were also routine eye and hearing tests, and visits from the school dentist. Class sizes in the early 1960s were large, often over 30 children to a class, as these were the 'baby boomers', children born after the Second World War. There were no classroom assistants, just the class teacher and discipline was strict. It was quite common for a disruptive child to be rapped over the knuckles, on the buttocks or on the palm of the hand with a ruler.

A Christmas party at a school in Wales

Background

After the Second World War, the state funded secondary education system was divided using a Tripartite system containing grammar schools, secondary technical colleges and secondary modern schools. The Eleven-plus examination was used to select which pupils went to which schools based on ability. As technical colleges were not available on the scale envisaged the exam came to symbolise fierce competition for places at the prestigious grammar schools. The very name still deeply divides opinion with many believing it was the symbol of a segregated two-tier school system whilst for others it set the educational benchmark.

Here's your chance to test yourself with example questions from the 1960s:
(Answers on page 92)

Arithmetic Questions

Question One: A train leaves London at 10:30am and arrives at Birmingham at 12:40pm. It stopped from 12:10pm to 12:20pm at Coventry which is 100 miles from London. It travelled both parts of the journey at the same rate. Find the distance from London to Birmingham.

Question Two: If 1st December falls on a Monday, on what day will Christmas Day fall that year?

Question Three: A machine makes toy soldiers at the rate of 75 in 5 minutes. How long with it take to make 6,000 of them? (answer in hours and minutes)

Question Four: Write in figures the sum of four hundred and forty six and seventy-seven.

Question Five: John is 12 years old and his mother is 42. Answer the following:

A) How old was John's mother when she was 4 times as old as him?

B) In how many years' time will his mother be three times as old as John?

C) How old will John be when his mother is 10 times as old as he was 6 years ago?

General English Questions

Question One: Change all necessary words to make these sentences plural:

A) My dog is carrying a stick.

B) His butcher has no meat.

C) A man who likes football is sure to have a team scarf in his house.

Question Two: Fill in the blank with a suitable missing word:

A) As *toe* is to *foot* so is .... to *hand*.

B) As *referee* is to *football* so is .... to *tennis*

C) As *Spain* is to .... so is *France* to *Frenchmen*

Question Three: Rewrite each of these sentences replacing the underlined words with a single word:

A) I was <u>in no doubt</u> that the shop would be closed.

B) He said that he would be coming home <u>in a short time</u>.

C) She <u>made up her mind</u> to go the cinema.

Top 10 Girls' Baby Names [1]

1. Susan — of Hebrew origin meaning "Lily Rose"
2. Julie — of French/Latin origin meaning "Youthful"
3. Karen — of Danish origin possibly via Ancient Greek Katharos meaning "Pure"
4. Jaqueline — from Hebrew via French meaning "may God protect"
5. Deborah — derived from the Hebrew word D'vorah meaning "Bee"
6. Tracey — from French and Gaelic Irish meaning "higher" or "superior"
7. Jane — from the Hebrew meaning "God is Merciful"
8. Helen — possibly from the Greek Selene meaning "Moon"
9. Diane — from Latin via French meaning "Divine"
10. Sharon — from Hebrew meaning "of the fertile plain"

Top 10 Boys' Baby Names [2]

1. David — corruption of the Hebrew name *Dawid* meaning "beloved"
2. Paul — from Latin meaning "Small" or "Humble"
3. Andrew — of Greek origin meaning "Garland or crown"
4. Mark — from the Latin name Mart-kos "consecrated to the god Mars"
5. John — of Hebrew origin meaning "God is Gracious"
6. Michael — of Hebrew origin meaning "One who is like God"
7. Stephen — of origin meaning "garland or crown"
8. Ian — a variation of John meaning "God is Gracious"
9. Robert — from the Old German meaning "Fame Bright"
10. Richard — from Old German meaning "Powerful leader"

[1] [2] Data compiled by the Office for National Statistics 1964

Games, Toys and Pastimes

Tipped as the toy of the year, Airtoy's spinning satellite was brought out to cash in on the growing fascination with space. Unfortunately it bore little resemblance to a real satellite other than spinning and lighting up, so once the initial batteries had run out it was usually binned. Corgi launched a model of Silverstone racetrack, replete with pit stops. Dinky brought out a toy model of the iconic American limousine, the Ford Fairlane. In America, Barbie and her boyfriend Ken were big sellers and in Britain, Dinky released a fire engine with flashing lights. Board and card games were popular seeing families gather round, and perhaps fall out, over a game of Monopoly, Cluedo or Happy Families. The first computer game, Spacewar!, was developed in 1962 at the Massachusetts Institute of Technology. Its graphics were basic and the computer it ran on was the size of a car. Children would have to wait more than ten years for Atari to bring out Pong, a simple game based on table tennis. The quantum leap forward came in 1977 with the introduction of Space Invaders. All in all toys were simpler and relied on the child's imagination to make them fun.

1960s Barbie doll

Relaxing in the front room this family has chosen some of the design trends that would come to define home furnishing in the 1960s. Despite the black and white photo it is clear to see the bold patterns on the sitting room chairs. The clashing patterns and vivid colours that would dominate the latter half of the 1960s were already evident in 1962 as consumers with increasing disposable income aspired to make over their austere post-war home interiors.

The trend for clean lines and functional design was most obvious in the kitchen with the rise of fitted cabinetry and integrated appliances.

With television programming for children limited to the odd programme per day, children would still spend most of their indoor time reading, drawing and playing games sat either at the dining table or on the floor in the lounge.

Record players were the mainstay of entertainment in most households. Here we see a father about to play an EP (extended play) record for his boys. EP's were a popular format in the UK until the late sixties.

In the bathroom homeowners were keen to modernise and update the layout to include fitted baths, vanity sink units and close coupled toilets. The picture above shows a lady cleaning the bath with an integrated shower attachment.

Children lucky enough to live in houses with a good sized garden would spend hours playing outdoors building dens, creating adventures and enjoying picnics. However, the park and the street were just as popular.

Design Trends in the Early Sixties

With increasing living standards and demand for modern home interiors the 1960s were a fertile time for design. British designers were making waves on the global stage as manufacturers invested in product development and aesthetic design. New materials and manufacturing techniques gave greater freedom to innovate. The trend saw sleek and streamlined furniture designs being complimented by patterned fabric textures and wall papers. With sustained economic growth during this period, British consumer confidence grew significantly as the public finally laid to rest the period of post-war shortages and austerity. This confidence was most obviously expressed in the increasing use of vivid colours in the home whether that be the carpets, the furniture or the wall coverings. Consumerism was most definitely on the rise. In the fifties, ownership of home appliances such as fridges or televisions was the preserve of the privileged few but by the early sixties it became the norm.

Whilst British design was gaining favour globally, the most influential design trends were emanating from the USA, Italy and Scandinavia. The Mid-Century Modern design movement in the USA was popular from 1945 to 1969. Its hallmarks were clean, simple lines and honest use of materials. Similar in ethos was the Scandinavian design movement which started to flourish in the 1950s. At its heart were the principles of simplicity, minimalism and functionality. Although the United Kingdom would have to wait until 1987 before seeing its first store open, the behemoth that is IKEA, founded by Ingvar Kamprad, was growing and developing in Sweden in 1962 and soon to expand to nearby Norway in 1963.

When in 1960 Elizabeth David produced her greatest work *French Provincial Cooking*, the Observer newspaper noted: "It is difficult to think that any home can do without it." By 1962 it had found its way onto the bookshelves of many homes around the country. By following her recipes British home cooks had embraced flavour and rescued culinary tastes from the bland Victorian fare prescribed by Mrs Beeton, whose recipes included an instruction to cook pasta for one and a half hours. David's path to domestic goddess status was an unorthodox one. She was born into an upper class family and came out as a debutante in 1932, but none of the men she met at various balls appealed to her. She then tried her hand at art and acting, both without much enthusiasm. It was while appearing with fellow actress Anna Neagle, that Neagle noted the young David did not even know how to make a cup of

tea. When David's family suspected her of having an affair with a married man, they packed her off to the continent. It was there that she not only embraced the culture, but immersed herself in the cuisine. The resultant cookery books and humorous journals would change British tastes forever.

A Classic Gratin Dauphinois Recipe (Serves 6)

Ingredients

- 2 lbs Desiree Potatoes (which had been bred in the Netherlands in 1962. However, King Edwards will do)
- 10 fl oz full fat milk
- 10 fl oz double cream
- 2 oz butter
- 1 garlic clove, peeled and halved
- 2 sprigs of fresh thyme, plus extra for sprinkling
- 1 shallot, roughly chopped (although a small onion would do)
- A pinch of finely grated nutmeg
- 1 oz freshly grated parmesan (a hard British cheese could also be used)
- Salt and pepper to taste

Method: Preheat the oven to Gas mark 4/ 160 degrees. Rub the butter all over the inside of a large shallow dish (about 18 by 11 inches). Peel and thinly slice the potatoes (approx 1/8" thick). Lay the slices on a tea towel and pat them dry. Keep them covered while preparing the rest of the ingredients. Pour the milk and cream into a saucepan. Add the garlic, thyme and shallot. Slowly warm the milk until just before it boils and then remove from the heat. Strain the liquid into a large jug and sprinkle with nutmeg. Layer about half the potatoes in the dish and season. Pour over half the milk and cream. Repeat with the remaining ingredients. Scatter the cheese over the top and bake for around an hour, when the potatoes should be tender and the topping golden brown. Leave to stand for 5 minutes and sprinkle over the remaining thyme. Bon appetit.

In the early 1960s pudding made up a substantial part of most meals, be it at school or in the home. Some were fulsomely enjoyed and have stayed firm favourites, whilst others have not. Although the food producer Ambrosia had resumed production of both tinned rice and tinned macaroni puddings after the war, it was more common for them to be home-made. Other favourite puddings included jam roly-poly, chocolate sponge with chocolate sauce, apple crumble, bread and butter pudding and blancmange. Acquired tastes included sago and tapioca puddings. There was also the pudding that made schoolboys giggle, Spotted Dick, which was also known as spotted dog or railway cake, which avoided double entendres.

Spotted Dick Recipe   (Serves 8)

Ingredients

- 10 oz self-raising flour
- 5 oz shredded suet
- 6 oz currants
- 4 oz caster sugar
- 2 oz mixed dried peel
- ¼ pint of milk, plus 3 tablespoons
- A pinch of salt

Method: Put the flour and salt into a mixing bowl. Add the suet, currants, sugar and mixed peel. Pour in the milk and mix to a firm but moist dough, adding extra milk if necessary. Shape into a fat roll about 8 inches long and wrap loosely in baking parchment, tying both ends with string, This will allow the pudding to rise. Place a steamer over a large pan of boiling water, add the wrapped pudding to the steamer and cook for 1½ hours. Check periodically whether the saucepan has run dry. Top up with water if necessary. Remove the pudding from the steamer and allow to cool slightly before unwrapping. Serve with custard.

Summer Holidays in 1962

In 1962 there were more choices on where to spend your hard-earned cash on a once-a-year holiday than ever before. At the top end was the growing cruise ship market. Choices included the recently launched SS Canberra. At 45,000 tons it was the largest vessel to pass through the Panama Canal to date. Competing at the luxury end of the market was the SS France, replete with two on-board swimming pools. European sun-soaked holidays were beginning to take off. In 1957 British European

The SS Canberra was an ocean liner in the P&O fleet

The swimming pool at Butlin's Pwllheli

Airways (BEA) had introduced a route to Alicante in Eastern Spain. The term Costa Blanca was created to promote it. However, a ferry was still a more affordable way to travel with popular destinations including France, Belgium, Holland and Ireland. Most people still holidayed at home. There were many options: the holiday camps (Warner, Butlin's or Pontins), an independently run caravan park, a bed and breakfast by the sea or simply staying with a relative down by the coast. For some people all the fun of the fair came to them, be it in the form of the Highland Games in Scotland, the Grasmere Games in the Lake District or the Eisteddfod in Wales. One particular event took place in Corby. The Corby Pole Fair is the most peculiar of British institutions. The fair possibly dates back to the 14th century and is held just once every 20 years. At its centre is a greasy pole which revellers attempt to climb to lay claim to a ham. In 1962, the festival-goers did not have to wait the full two decades as the 1942 incarnation was delayed until 1947 because of the war.

Enjoying the Eisteddfod festival in Wales

A family camping trip was a popular summer holiday choice

Radio Butlin was an integral part of the Butlin's camp experience, as immortalised in the TV sitcom Hi-De-Hi.

Campers were assigned into 'Houses' for all the sports, games and competitions. Rivalry was friendly but intense!

The Ladies Dancing competition was judged with points for the winner going towards their House total.

The inter-house Tug of War competition was particularly competitive. It drew big crowds cheering the teams on.

Children's entertainer, Uncle Boko, is pictured here presenting the "Father and Son" competition.

Redcoats would be assigned to tables to eat with campers to continue the Butlin's experience through mealtimes.

The houndstooth coat was a popular fashion item in 1962. The tessellated pattern of broken checks was most commonly black and white but other colour combinations were available, including dark red/white.

At a youth fashion show, the model is wearing a polo neck and checkered trousers. Note the fashionable hairstyles in the room!

Riding a Vespa scooter, this model is wearing a light-coloured polo neck jumper with tartan waistcoat over and matching capri pants.

This yoke-top shift dress, complete with matching jacket, has a naval feel.

Christmas 1962

In many ways the Christmases of the early 1960's were very similar to that of today. Families gathered together and shared much laughter and fun. But whereas today the celebrations often centre around lavish presents and the use of social media, then the celebrations were much more home made. Greeting cards would be sent to all members of the family and it was very often the only written communication of the year. Some would contain news of the past year including news of how well the children were doing at school or in sports. In 1962 the telephone bore a greater resemblance to a table lamp than the devices of today. Calls were brief with salutations and felicitations being exchanged, all the time keeping an eye on the cost. The days of post-war rationing were still all too recent memories so Christmas had a more frugal feel compared to today. Decorations were simple and improvised.

Tucking in to Christmas treats

Visiting Santa at his grotto

Brightly coloured paper chains were made by the family and strung across the walls in the living room. If money was tight, these could be made from strips of wallpaper. Children's TV programme Blue Peter was at hand to show you how to make your own decorations. Many of these defied health and safety standards, including how to make an advent crown from wire coat hangers, with a lit candle at each end! Food preparation began weeks, if not months in advance. The fruit for the pudding would be steeped in alcohol, and when ready would be stirred into the batter along with a silver sixpence for luck. Few people had home freezers, so all the components of the Christmas lunch had to be purchased as close as possible to the big day. Members of the family were sent out to all four corners of the town or village to collect orders from the butcher, greengrocer and the baker as supermarkets were in their infancy. On Christmas Eve, parents would prepare a feast of mince pies and sherry (whisky in Scotland) for Father Christmas, which would disappear by morning. Sometimes a carrot would also be left for Rudolph. Children left stockings or pillow cases by their beds ready to be filled with gifts, but only if they had been good, of course! Main presents were opened after breakfast: for children these might be a watch (perhaps a Tic-a-Tic-a-Timex), Scalextric or a Sindy doll. Other favourite gifts included Etch-a-Sketch, Meccano, 3D View Master and the Amazing Magic Robot that answered questions. Relatives might also bring home made gifts, such as hand knitted jumpers and scarves. As there were no shops open on Christmas Day, the words "batteries not included" led to an occasional tearful afternoon as shops would not reopen until after Boxing Day. The day itself was one of indulgence. Very often a full English breakfast was served in the morning. The dinner itself was not always turkey as, often, the meat of choice might be chicken or goose. The best tablecloth, china, glasses and silverware were brought out for this most special of occasions, before being packed away for another year.

A festive family portrait around the tree

1962 was a pivotal year for the British film industry. A whole host of major films were released which would go on to become timeless classics. *Lawrence of Arabia*, including the iconic scene where Peter O'Toole in the titular role emerges slowly from the desert riding a camel, was the outstanding film of the year. It was also the highest grossing film of the year and gained seven Oscars. The US Library of Congress Film Registry preserved the film for its cultural and historical importance. The year also saw the first James Bond film, *Dr. No*. It was based on the sixth Ian Fleming book of the series (*Casino Royale* being the first). It starred Sean Connery as 007, with a supporting cast

Peter O'Toole as Lawrence of Arabia

including Ursula Andress, Joseph Wiseman and Jack Lord. The film, though panned by some critics, was a huge commercial success despite its minuscule budget. It also contains probably the most iconic Bond scene when a bikini-clad Andress emerges from the ocean. In America, The National Broadcasting Company was at its most innovative, screening productions of *Spellbound* and *Rebecca* starring Maureen O'Hara and James Mason respectively. In Britain, the highlight of the theatrical year was Peter Brook's innovative and demanding RSC production of King Lear, starring Paul Scofield as the troubled ruler. The first night of the Promenade season started with Benjamin Britten's *The Young Person's Guide to the Orchestra* and finished with Henry Wood's *Fantasia on British Sea Songs*. The season climax was loaded with patriotism as the crowd sang *Rule Britannia. Land of Hope and Glory*, followed by *God Save the Queen*.

Henry Wood

1962 was a curious year for music. The sixties, as we think of them, hadn't yet really begun. The Beatles released their first single *Love Me Do*, but it only reached number 17 in the charts. The Rolling Stones performed their first live gig, but only as a last minute stand-in and

Cliff Richard

David Bowie was still at art college. Traditional jazz, informally known as trad jazz, was big with Acker Bilk, Chris Barber and Kenny Ball leading the way. The spending power was still with the older population and record sales reflected this. Many of the top-sellers were songs from the musicals. Soundtracks from *West Side Story*, *The King and I*, *South Pacific* and *Oliver!* were all top 10 hits. From across the Atlantic, Elvis Presley and Frank Sinatra were both in their heyday whilst Bobby Vee and Ray

The Rolling Stones

Charles both had hits in the UK. On the home front Cliff Richard and the Shadows both topped the charts. One group who enjoyed enormous success in the charts that sticks out like a sore thumb is the George Mitchell Minstrels, a blackface parody of black American music, now thankfully socially unacceptable. For most young people, they chose to listen to alternative radio stations including Radio Luxembourg and Radio Hilversum as they found the BBC Light Service too staid.

Whatever Happened to Baby Jane

Starring Bette Davis and Joan Crawford
Directed by Robert Aldrich
Released October 31st 1962

The tension between the two protagonists in the movie is palpable, but it was nothing compared to the enmity the two stars had for each other off the screen. Bette Davis and Joan Crawford hated each other. The film starts in 1917 where 6-year-old Jane Hudson (Davis) is a successful Vaudeville performer. Fast-forward to 1935 and her sister Blanche (Crawford) is paralysed in a car accident for which Jane is held responsible. What ensues is a terrifying psychological thriller with dark comedic moments as the sadistic Jane holds Blanche prisoner in the upstairs of their mansion. Many of the scenes of violence had to be cut in order for it to be passed for even adult viewing in the UK. Many present on set testified that much of the violence was real. The feud was believed to have started when Crawford announced her divorce from Douglas Fairbanks Jr. on the day of Davis' film premiere of 1935's *Ex-Lady*. The film flopped. It also didn't help that Hollywood's two leading ladies of the era often competed for the same roles. Crawford also stole Davis' lover Franchot Tone, and to compound matters won an Oscar for her role in *Mildred Pierce* in 1945; a role Davis had turned down. When Crawford died of a heart attack in 1977, Davis was quoted as saying, "You should never say bad things about the dead, only good.....Joan Crawford is dead. Good."

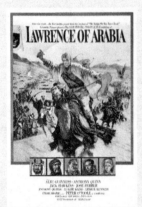

Lawrence of Arabia

Starring Peter O'Toole, Omar Sharif and Alec Guinness
Directed by David Lean
Released December 10th 1962

The film is a sweeping, epic and literate version of British adventurer and soldier T.E. Lawrence's experiences in Arabia during the First World War. Lawrence, perfectly played by Peter O'Toole, goes "native" when he is sent into the desert to find Prince Feisal (Alec Guinness). Lawrence is soon striking out against the Ottoman Empire, which still held sway in the region at the time. His efforts to unify the various Arab factions are particularly prescient. He becomes an inspirational warlord whose neutral presence amongst the Arab tribes, lead by El Kharish (Omar Sharif) and Abu Tayi (Anthony Quinn), serves to glue together uneasy alliances. As well as wrestling with his own demons and the cruel desert environment, the Englishman is also faced with culture clashes which pit not only the imperialists against the indigenous populations, but also Arab guerrillas against the discipline of the British army. In the end, Lawrence himself does not know which side he is on, nor which party he belongs to. Set against a backdrop of the Arabian desert, the nomadic allies, under Lawrence's direction, attack and disrupt the Turks' efforts to maintain control whilst the British army pushes ever deeper into the area. Not until his job is done does Lawrence learn that the French and British governments have carved up the middle-east between them.

The Longest Day

Richard Burton

Starring John Wayne, Richard Burton, Henry Fonda and Robert Ryan
Directed by Ken Annakin (British and French) Andrew Marton (American)
Released September 25th 1962

In 1962 the Second World War was still fresh in the memory. This film sought to document the events surrounding its pivotal moment, the Normandy Landings. It was made on an epic scale featuring an all-star cast from Britain, America and Germany. It was most remarkable for its even-handed portrayal of ordinary soldiers from both sides of the conflict. It comprehensively details the build-up to the invasion of mainland Europe by allied forces in 1944, taking care to show how the battle was perceived by both allied and axis soldiers and generals. Unlike other movies of the genre, it doesn't lapse into sentimentality and is free from the distraction of fictionalised characters' personal lives. It is for many the ultimate film about war and the last great war film to be shot in black and white. The overhead shots of the Normandy Beaches give you an idea of the scale of the movie, with hundreds of tanks and landing craft giving an accurate picture of the enormity of the invasion. The only thing that detracts from the film is that the cast was full of too many big stars with competing egos. Whilst this multi-star format worked with lighter films like *Towering Inferno*, in *The Longest Day* it stopped the film knitting together. In the Oscars of the following year it was nominated for best picture, but received no nominations in any of the acting categories.

Cape Fear

Peck and Bergen

Starring Gregory Peck and Robert Mitchum
Directed by J. Lee Thompson
Released April 12th 1962

Few actors could do menace as well as Robert Mitchum, and in *Cape Fear* he is at his menacing best. Gregory Peck plays a happily married lawyer, Sam Bowden, whose life is turned upside down when Max Cady (Robert Mitchum) is released from an eight year prison sentence. Cady blames Bowden for his incarceration for a nasty assault, so sets out to persecute the whole family. Once Bowden realises that Cady is hell-bent on revenge and that his family are in serious danger, he turns to the police for help. When that help from the justice system is not forthcoming, he is forced to go outside of the law. Soon all parties are heading towards a dark and dangerous place. That place is Cape Fear. Gregory Peck co-produced the movie and felt he needed a co-star of equal status to act alongside him. It is a testament to Peck's generosity that he showed no sign of jealousy when Mitchum got all the plaudits. The decision to shoot in black and white was also inspired, adding to the tension that dripped from every frame. Polly Bergen plays Bowden's wife and Lori Morgan his daughter; there is also an appearance from Telly Savalas, before he sported his trademark bald head. That the film received no major Oscar nominations owes more to the internal politics of Hollywood than the merits of the movie. It goes down as one of the greatest film noirs of all time.

Sean Connery as 007

Dr. No

Starring Sean Connery, Ursula Andress and Joseph Wiseman
Directed by Terence Young
Released October 5th 1962

1962 is the year we first welcomed James Bond to the big screen. We found out that he liked fast cars, gadgets, the company of beautiful women and getting into tight scrapes with evil warlords. Although the writer of the Bond series of books, Ian Fleming, wanted the debonair English actor David Niven to take the role, Scotsman Sean Connery was chosen. For many, his is the ultimate Bond; tall, handsome and laid back. In this first film, James Bond of the British Secret Service is sent to Jamaica to investigate the suspicious death of an operative named Strangeway. He learns that the operative had been looking into alarmingly high radiation emissions from a nearby island, Crab Cay. Bond heads to the island only to find it heavily fortified, patrolled by gunmen, vicious dogs and gunboats. The locals believe the island to be guarded by a dragon. Undeterred Bond, with the aid of a Jamaican agent called Quarrel (John Kitzmiller) and a diver called Honey Ryder (Ursula Andress), heads toward the island. They discover that it is run by Dr. No (Joseph Wiseman), a megalomaniac with plans to disrupt the US space programme. Needless to say Bond does what Bond does best: outwitting the evil genius, but not before getting captured and meeting near certain death. In the end he emerges shaken, not stirred, like his favourite drink.

Carry on Cruising

Directed by Gerald Thomas
Starring Sid James, Kenneth Williams, Liz Fraser et al.
Released April 13th 1962

Although it is missing some of the regular Carry On crew, most notably Joan Sims and Charles Hawtrey, the movie is one of the best of the series. Tapping in to the growing trend for cruise holidays, the script is sharp with some great gags delivered by the ensemble. Sid James plays the world-weary and experienced captain of a cruise liner in charge of a largely inexperienced crew. This is the perfect setup for a series of disasters that the film duly delivers.

The fact that *Carry on Cruising* was the first Carry On to be filmed in colour, gives the film a freshness lacking in some of the previous outings. The newer cast members keep the mix interesting and there are standout performances from Esma Cannon who plays a lonely but happy spinster. The bar scene with Dilys Lane where both their characters get outrageously drunk is one of the highlights of the film. Those who prefer the earlier Carry On films, may find this one falling between two stools. But, as always though, it provides enough real laughs and remains as good-natured and watchable as any in the series. A good example of vintage British humour.

The Saint

Roger Moore as The Saint

Starring Roger Moore, Campbell Singer and Ivor Dean
Ran from October 4th 1962 to February 9th 1969

Adapted from a highly successful series of books by Leslie Charteris, the character Simon Templar was propelled on to our screens by the oh-so suave, handsome and debonair Roger Moore. The role was originally offered to Patrick McGoohan, who at the time was playing secret agent John Drake in *Danger Man* (1960-67), but the final choice of Roger Moore proved perfect. The weekly show saw Templar, aka *The Saint* (from his initials ST) frequenting fashionable bars, enjoying the company of beautiful women and fighting underworld criminals in defence of the vulnerable. Smartly dressed and every inch the ladies' man, he came to represent the perfect English gentleman. The programme's release came at a time when British culture was on the verge of conquering the world. The Beatles were about to take America by storm and the Britpop art movement was about to take off. All of this made *The Saint* and Moore a huge international success. Whilst the programme may have seemed light and frothy, it was the mystery surrounding the character of Simon Templar that sustained its appeal. The viewers were offered no backstory about the enigmatic Saint including the means by which he maintained such a luxurious lifestyle. The recurring character Chief Inspector Teal clearly believed that it was acquired by illegal means, although he never managed to prove it. *The Saint* managed to stay in pursuit of criminals whilst keeping one step ahead of the law.

Z-Cars

Brian Blessed in Z-Cars

Starring James Ellis, Brian Blessed, Stratford Johns and Frank Windsor
Created by Troy Kennedy Martin
First aired 2nd January 1962

By 1962, the once groundbreaking *Dixon of Dock Green* (1955-76) had become out-dated. Its world of low-level criminality, gentleman rogues, wayward youths and easily solved crimes was seen as too cosy. This was especially as each episode ended with the avuncular Dixon delivering a reassuring homily over a nice cup of tea. Something more hard-hitting was called for, and it arrived in the shape of Troy Kennedy Martins's *Z-Cars*. Set in the fictional northern satellite town of Newton and its neighbour Seaport, it took British police drama to another level. It portrayed the police as sometimes less-than-perfect individuals. The very first episode featured an officer who was a compulsive gambler, with another who was a domestic abuser. The criminals were a mixture of low-life villains, small-time gangsters, pimps, muggers and corrupt landlords. The series was gritty and issue-driven, never shying away from real-world problems such as poverty, racism, drug addiction and mental illness. Like most series of the time, it was shot "live" but also featured many filmed inserts, which gave it a more convincing appearance of reality. *Z-Cars* was truly groundbreaking, both in its subject matter and in the way it was made. British police drama owes a great debt to Martin and the cast who propelled the genre into the second half of the twentieth century.

Bamber Gascoigne

University Challenge

Quiz master: Bamber Gascoigne

First aired 21st September 1962 on ITV

University Challenge is a quiz where the rules are simple and the questions are anything but. A starter question for ten points, if answered correctly, gains a team three supplementary questions each worth five points. A wrong answer given before the question has been completed incurs a five point penalty. The original programme was presided over by the bespectacled, unflappable Bamber Gascoigne, himself a religious scholar. The format was simple: two teams (of four students each) representing different universities were pitted against each other in a race to buzz first. It asked the most difficult questions of any TV quiz and often had viewers astonished by the range of the scholars' knowledge. The show, however, was not without controversy. Oxford and Cambridge were allowed to compete as individual colleges, whereas other universities could only enter one team each. Polytechnics were also excluded from the show. The first series which had its final in 1963 was won by the University of Leicester which was only given University status six years earlier. They beat Balliol College Oxford (founded in 1263), which put a dampener on their 700th anniversary celebrations. Early contestants who went on to be famous included former Irish President Mary Robinson (1966), journalist John Simpson (1964) and actress Miriam Margolyes (1963). The show gradually fell out of favour, with some viewers seeing it as elitist. It also looked increasingly out of place on commercial TV. It was eventually cancelled in 1987. It was revived in 1994 by BBC2 with new host, Jeremy Paxman.

TW3 Opening Titles

That Was the Week That Was

Presenter: David Frost

Cast: Millicent Martin; Kenneth Cope; Roy Kinnear; Bernard Levin et al.

That Was the Week That Was, which quickly became known as TW3, was a daring satirical look at current affairs featuring sketches, humorous songs and parodies of the news. However, the programme that was the first to bring satire to British televisions almost didn't appear at all. The BBC commissioned a pilot of the show but had concerns about lampooning their political masters. After all, it was in the power of politicians to renew or end the BBC's licence. Word spread that the newly created ITV (commercial television) were about to poach Frost and steal the show's format, so TW3 was quickly given the green light by the BBC. Frost presented as if born to the format with the show becoming an instant success. The studio set up was enormously influential for future television with previously hidden scaffolding and cameras clearly on show, all of which added to the edginess of TW3. The show also gained from being in the right place at the right time. Prime Minister Harold Macmillan, who had previously been portrayed as "SuperMac", was beginning to see his world crumble around him. A disastrous Cabinet reshuffle, dubbed the "Night of the Long Knives" and the later sex scandal, the Profumo affair, gave the team much to work with. Macmillan was laid back about TW3, however, in 1963 the BBC's cold feet resurfaced and they pulled the show. In its short life, *That Was the Week That Was* had changed the landscape of TV forever.

Animal Magic

Presenters: Johnny Morris, Gerald Durrell, Tony Soper
First aired April 13th 1962

Johnny Morris

Johnny Morris was the voice of children's radio and gained television fame as the storyteller, the Hot Chestnut Man, in BBC's *Playbox* which ran from 1955-64. When Desmond Hawkins was charged with setting up a Natural History Unit at the BBC, he wanted to create a programme specially for children. He turned to naturalist Gerald Durrell, ornithologist Tony Soper and, in a stroke of genius, Morris who had no scientific training but was an excellent communicator. Durrell and Soper filmed mainly out in the field usually in Pembrokeshire, leaving Morris with more exotic animals in Bristol Zoo. In the very first episode, Morris had an encounter with a woolly monkey who climbed on his head while he was delivering a piece to camera. The unflappable Morris incorporated the monkey's high jinks into the recording and the tone was set for the next twenty years. Throughout the series Morris made nature accessible to children by dubbing different voices to all the animals. He was a brilliant mimic and always seemed to find the appropriate voice for each animal. A hippo would be given a low rumbling voice whilst a monkey would have a shrill, piercing delivery. Despite two naturalists being involved, it was Morris who stole the show with his very unscientific way of "communicating" with the animals. The show's strength eventually became its weakness when Johnny's whimsical eccentricity disappeared from our screens in 1983 as BBC bosses thought it not educational enough.

Steptoe and Son

Starring Wilfred Brambell and Harry H. Corbett
Created by Ray Galton and Alan Simpson
First aired 7th June 1962

Harold and Albert Steptoe

At its best, *Steptoe and Son* resembles a Samuel Beckett play. Harold Steptoe lived with his father Albert in West London where they ran a rag and bone business. Harold yearned for a better life, but Albert liked life as it was, constantly thwarting his son's ambitions. The series established a template for the British sitcom in its purest form. Each episode had a similar theme. Harold and Albert would be sharing a miserable existence but then a threat to the status quo occurred, usually when Harold met a woman or pursued some kind of artistic pipe dream. *Steptoe and Son* breaks down the boundaries between comedy and tragedy. The family bond is presented as a psychological prison. Albert is a comedic monster, persistently undermining Harold to maintain control. The pain is compounded by the fact that despite his airs and graces, Harold is far less intelligent than his wily "dirty old man" father.

The show was the most popular comedy of its day. By the mid-1960s, over half the population watched it. In 1966 the Prime Minister, Harold Wilson, pressured the BBC into moving the transmission time as he feared it would adversely affect the turnout of Labour voters.

The biggest event in British radio in 1962 was one that could not be heard by the public, but would eventually change the way we listened to radio forever. In June, the Pilkington Committee on Broadcasting published a report that would devolve BBC radio to the regions. Fearful of the impending creation of local commercial radio, the nation's broadcaster hoped to get a head start. Trial closed-circuit broadcasts began almost immediately. In the meantime the British public had to make do with three services, little changed since the time of the Second World War. The Home Service, which evolved from the pre-war National Programme, featured news, entertainment and magazine programmes such as *Woman's Hour*. This was later to become Radio 4. The Light Programme, launched in 1945, featured jazz and easy listening music as well as sport and light entertainment. This was to become Radio 2. The Third Programme was the most highbrow of the three, playing classical music, this eventually became Radio 3. The only notable radio debut was

Broadcasting House in London

The Men from the Ministry, an irreverent look at the civil service, starring Wilfred Hyde-White and Richard Murdoch. Instead, audiences listened to ongoing shows, some of which have endured to this day. *Farming Today, The Archers, Any Questions?* and *In Touch* can still be heard. Other programmes seemed tired and staid and were soon to run their course. *Music while you Work, Housewife's Choice* and *Mrs Dale's Diary* spoke more to an older generation than the baby boomers of the day. For pre-school children there was always *Listen With Mother*. Sport also featured prominently with *Test Match Special* bringing painterly descriptions of England cricket matches from around the globe. Silky-voiced poet and cricket-lover John Arlott was the greatest of the commentators. The BBC was also keen on real-life outside broadcasts; *Down Your Way*, a programme that toured the towns and villages of the UK, was hugely popular. What was sorely lacking in the Corporation's output was programming aimed at the youth market. *Pick of the Pops* and *Easy Beat* were two shows that catered for the young, but there was precious little else. In America, 1962 saw the end of the Golden Age of Radio. September 30th saw the final broadcasts of the long-running

Letter from America with Alistair Cooke

drama serials *Suspense* and *Yours Truly, Johnny Dollar*. A broadcasting medium that had once played host to Orson Welles, T.S. Eliot and Chekov had finally lost the battle to television. Advertisers switched their funding with radio in the States becoming more music and news based, suitable for listening to when driving along in your automobile. One programme which bridged the Atlantic and became compulsory listening for many was Alistair Cooke's *Letter from America*. In a world far less interconnected than today, Cooke would broadcast weekly from his adopted New York. His broadcasts would range from idle conversations with his local bar owner to urgent matters of the day. In 1962, the Cuban Missile Crisis featured large; Cooke provided a reassuringly familiar voice from across the pond. It was radio at its simplest and its best.

Twist and Shout

Performed by The Isley Brothers

Written By Bert Berns (under the pseudonym Bert Russell) and Phil Medley

Released in the summer of 1962

Original record label

Twist and Shout was a slow burner of a song. It was first recorded in February 1961 by the group The Top Notes, but was not released as a single until the Autumn as a B-side to, *Always Late (Why Lead Me On)*. The original song was produced by Phil Spector, but the head of Atlantic Records was not happy with his version. Songwriter Berns took the song to the Isley Brothers and persuaded them to record it, this time doing the production himself. The result was a Number 1 R&B hit. The song later became famous in the UK when the Beatles recorded it in 1963 on their album *Please Please Me*. The Beatles' version was not released as a single in the UK, but peaked at number 2 in the US Billboard Hot Hundred.

I Remember You

Performed by Frank Ifield

Written by Victor Schertzinger with lyrics by Johnny Mercer

Released June 29th 1962

Frank Ifield

1962 was a pivotal year for music. The Beatles were taking Hamburg by storm, Elvis was producing hit after hit and the Rolling Stones played their first concert. Yet one of the biggest selling singles of the year was *I Remember You*, which featured yodelling. Written at the height of the Second World War, it spoke more to the older generation than the up-and-coming teenage market. The song did however sell over 1 million copies in the UK alone and stayed at number 1 for seven weeks. It also reached number 5 in the US charts. Although the song was often parodied, its bare lyrics express great love. "I remember you-ooh. You're the one who made my dreams come true, a few kisses ago!" *I Remember You* was the biggest selling single of 1962 in the UK.

Rockin' Around the Christmas Tree

Performed by Brenda Lee

Written by Johnny Marks

Released in the UK in December 1962

Brenda Lee

Johnny Marks had previously written *Rudolph the Red-Nosed Reindeer* and *A Holly Jolly Christmas*, so clearly had an eye for the lucrative Yuletide market. The choice of Brenda Lee to record the song in America in 1958 was a stroke of genius. Lee was only thirteen at the time, but had a far more grown-up singing voice. The combination was electric, her exuberant youth and a mature voice made the song one of the all-time great Christmas standards. The song has also been recorded by Bill Haley and the Comets, Kim Wilde and there was even a dance version by Italian DJ Gabry Ponte. Downloads have further fuelled the song's success. It has charted every Christmas since 2014.

Bob Dylan

Bob Dylan

By Bob Dylan

Released March 19th 1962

Nobel Laureate Bob Dylan's eponymous debut album was very similar to the first albums of the Rolling Stones and the Beatles. It stood above much that had gone before it, but was eclipsed by the artist's subsequent efforts. The album was released at the height of a folk/protest revival and largely featured songs written by other artists. The young Dylan, who was greatly influenced by Woody Guthrie, performs *Man of Constant Sorrow* and *Pretty Peggy-O* as if channelling his hero. In fact the album contained only two songs written by Dylan: *Talkin' New York* and *Song to Woody*. On other songs the influence of the black blues singers Blind Lemon Jefferson and Blind Willie Johnson can be heard. A year later, *The Freewheelin' Bob Dylan* was released featuring mostly original material including *Blowin' in the Wind* and *Masters of War*. These went on to be folk classics. Dylan had finally found his own voice.

Ray Charles

I Can't Stop Loving You

Sung by Ray Charles

Written by Don Gibson

Reached No.1 in the UK Singles Chart on July 12th 1962

The song was originally written and recorded by country singer Don Gibson in 1958 as the B-side of his hit single *Oh Lonesome Me*. Kitty Wells, who was a huge country star, also recorded the song and entered the charts at the same time as Gibson. But it is the Ray Charles version that is best remembered. Charles was already established as an R&B and gospel singer, but in a brave move decided to release a country album. His producer, Sid Feller, put together a tape of over 100 country songs so Charles could choose which ones to record. Included in the tapes was *I Can't Stop Loving You* which Charles remembered from listening to the Grand Ole Opry. For Charles, country music and R&B were a natural fit and his silky smooth rendition of this country staple was one of his biggest hits.

Bernard Cribbins

Right, Said Fred

Sung by Bernard Cribbins

Written by Ted Dicks and Myles Rudge

Released 29th June 1962

Bernard Cribbins had already established himself as a comic actor with roles in *Make Mine a Million* and *Two Way Stretch*, alongside the likes of Arthur Askey and Peter Sellers. In his third foray into music he narrated probably the most accomplished novelty record of all time. Produced by George Martin of Beatles fame, it is about three workmen who are moving an unnamed, but quite awkward, large object. Eventually after all but demolishing their customer's house, they give up and go home, or at least two of them do. Cribbins' comic timing brings the whole story of slack workmen and the trail of destruction they leave behind to life. In 1989 the Fairbrass brothers named their new band Right Said Fred after the song. Cribbins performed on their 1993 single *Stick It Out*, written for Comic Relief.

The Beatles

Love Me Do
By The Beatles. Written by John Lennon and Paul McCartney

Iris Caldwell may not be a household name, she changed British popular music forever. She was the object of Paul McCartney's affection when he and John Lennon skipped school to write *Love Me Do* in 1958. By 1962 The Beatles were playing in clubs in Hamburg performing covers of blues tunes by American artists. It caused quite a stir when they introduced an original song into their set. *Love Me Do* was well received and it gave the band confidence to write and perform their own material. The rest as they say is history. When they recorded the song in June 1962, Pete Best was on drums. Another version was recorded in September with Ringo holding the sticks. The version that was released on their first album *Please Please Me* had Andy White on drums, with a nervous Ringo playing the tambourine. The song reached No.17 in thc UK charts in 1962. During the height of Beatlemania, it gave the band their fourth US No.1 in 1964.

Cliff Richard

The Young Ones
Sung By Cliff Richard
Written by Sid Tepper and Roy Bennett

Cliff Richard had already tasted UK number 1 success with *Living Doll* and *Travellin' Light*, but it was *The Young Ones* that propelled him to stardom. It had been the title song for a film of the same name released the previous year, starring Cliff and Robert Morley. Like the film, the song told of teenage rebellion. Upon release it went straight to number 1. There were half a million advance orders and it would go on to sell over one million copies in the UK, and over two and a half million worldwide. It topped the charts in Australia, Denmark, Ireland, New Zealand and Israel. American singer Cathy Carroll released a cover version in the States, but it was met with a lukewarm reception. Even though the song was written by two Americans, its cosy portrayal of teenaged rebellion may have been a little too timid for their tastes.

Elvis Presley

Return to Sender
Sung by Elvis Presley
Written by Winfield Scott and Otis Blackwell

Elvis had three of the five best-selling singles of 1962. *Good Luck Charm*, *Can't Help Falling in Love* and the biggest of them all *Return to Sender*. The song tells the story of a lovers' spat, whilst taking the listener through the vagaries of the US postal system. It starts with a guy sending a letter to his love. She refuses to open it, instead writing "Return to sender, address unknown" on the envelope. The guy has a hard time believing that she does not want to read the letter, so he sends it special delivery. This is also returned unopened. He then decides that the third attempt should be hand delivered, which perhaps he should have done in the first place. We never find out the content of the letter or if the hand delivery works. Instead we are left in suspense when Elvis proclaims "If it comes back the very next day, I will understand."

Top of the Pops in 1962

There were 13 number one records in 1962 in the UK single charts published by the NME. The best selling single of the year was *I Remember You* by Frank Ifield .

		Weeks at number one
	Moon River / Danny Williams From 28th December 1961 for 2 weeks	‖
	The Young Ones / Cliff Richard and The Shadows From 11th January 1962 for 6 weeks	‖‖‖
	Can't Help Falling in Love / Elvis Presley From 22nd February 1962 for 4 weeks	‖‖
	Wonderful Land / The Shadows From 22nd March 1962 for 8 weeks	‖‖‖‖
	Nut Rocker / B. Bumble and the Stingers From 17th May 1962 for 1 week	‖
	Good Luck Charm / Elvis Presley From 24th May 1962 for 5 weeks	‖‖‖
	Come Outside / Mike Sarne with Wendy Richard From 28th June 1962 for 2 weeks	‖
	I Can't Stop Loving You / Ray Charles From 12th July 1962 for 2 weeks	‖
	I Remember You / Frank Ifield From 26th July 1962 for 7 weeks	‖‖‖‖
	She's Not You / Elvis Presley From 13th September 1962 for 3 weeks	‖‖
	Telstar / The Tornados From 4th October 1962 for 5 weeks	‖‖‖
	Lovesick Blues / Frank Ifield From 8th November 1962 for 5 weeks	‖‖‖
	Return to Sender / Elvis Presley From 13th December 1962 for 3 weeks	‖‖

The Rolling Stones' first live performance

July 12th 1962 at The Marquee Jazz Club, London

On a swelteringly hot July evening the Rolling Stones played their first gig. When Marquee Club regular Alexis Korner's band, Blues Incorporated, were offered a spot on BBC Radio's *Jazz Club* it left the venue with a hole to fill. Korner had a plan. He had made friends with a number of up-and-coming musicians, including a certain Mick Jagger and Keith Richards. Korner asked them to step in. Having landed the gig, Jagger's first ever interview with the press was carried by Jazz News, where he stated "I hope they don't think we are a rock 'n roll outfit." There was also the small matter of what the band should call themselves. It was decided that they should be called the Rolling Stones. There is much conjecture about how they chose the name. That it came from a Muddy Waters song isn't in doubt, but it is unlikely that the name came from the record *Rolling Stone Blues*. Dave Godin, a close friend of the band, explained that the record was only released on 78 rpm and they wouldn't be seen dead with one. Instead, the band probably got their name from the song *Mannish Blues*, released on EP, which contained the lyric "Ooo, I'm a rollin' stone." According to the handwritten set list, among the numbers they performed were songs by their heroes Jimmy Reed, Chuck Berry and Fats Domino. Songs included *Kansas City*, *Confessin' The Blues*, *Bright Lights Big City*, and *Dust My Broom*. Sixty years on, the world's greatest rock and roll band were still performing.

The Rolling Stones original lineup : Mick Jagger (top), Charlie Watts (centre left), Keith Richards (centre right), Brian Jones (bottom left) and Bill Wyman (bottom right)

The Marquee Club opened in 1958 in what used to be the Marquee Ballroom in the basement of the Academy Cinema in Oxford Street. Originally hosting jazz nights, it started regular R&B nights from 1962. It would go on to host a roll call of legendary acts including Muddy Waters, Led Zeppelin and The Who.

The Rolling Stones performing on stage early in their career

The Royal Variety Performance on October 29th 1962 at The London Palladium

in the presence of Her Majesty Queen Elizabeth II and His Royal Highness the Duke of Edinburgh

Hosted by Norman Vaughan, Queen Elizabeth II's tenth Royal Variety Performance brought together musical, comedic and theatrical talent from both sides of the Atlantic. There was singing from two female vocalists, Britain's Cleo Laine and America's Eartha Kitt. Comedy came in the form of Mike and Bernie Winters, Dickie Henderson and quick-fire gag man, Bob Hope. The surprise hit of the whole show was the amazing juggling of Rudy Cardenas. Eartha Kitt was disappointed when she was told that she could not direct her songs at the Royal Box. She later claimed not to sing naughty songs, but her whole career was based on purring sensuality; the Duke of Edinburgh may have been more disappointed than the Queen! Sophie Tucker, the last of the Red-Hot Mommas stole the show. She had first appeared a the Royal Variety Performance in 1922 in front of the queen's grandfather King George V. She recreated burlesque from a bygone era with her powerful delivery of comical and risqué songs. There were also appearances from the most successful British acts of the year, Cliff Richard and The Shadows, as well as plenty of yodelling from Frank Ifield. Music and mirth were combined in the form of Harry Secombe, who had only recently left the Goons. To misquote the Queen's great-great grandmother Queen Victoria, the royal couple (as well as the audience) left the Palladium most amused.

Host Norman Vaughan

British singer Cleo Laine

Sophie Tucker signing autographs

Cliff Richard and The Shadows

Singer Frank Ifield

Comedian Bob Hope

American singer Eartha Kitt

The Nobel Prize in Literature was awarded to John Steinbeck for his body of work. On this his eleventh nomination, the committee finally decided to give him literature's highest honour. Other nominees included Britain's Robert Graves and Lawrence Durrell. Steinbeck's writings were mostly about powerless people, often immigrants and their struggles during the Great Depression. His choice of titles reflected his eclectic reading tastes. *The Grapes of Wrath* is taken from the Book of Revelations, *Of Mice and Men* from Robert Burns' poem *To a Mouse* and *East of Eden*, which he considered his greatest work, mirrors much of the Book of Genesis. The Pulitzer Prize for non-fiction was won by Theodore White for *The Making of a President 1960*, which is widely regarded as the greatest book about John F. Kennedy written in his lifetime.

Nobel Laureate John Steinbeck

The year in poetry was eventful. In May, Benjamin Britten's *War Requiem* premiered at the newly consecrated Coventry Cathedral. In it he set the World War I poet Wilfred Owen's words to music in a magnificent, challenging and discordant opera. In September Ted Hughes and Silvia Plath, two of the leading poets of the day, ended their relationship. This immediately led to a burst of creativity from Plath, writing poems that would be published in the collections *Winter Trees* and *Ariel*, her greatest works. She tragically took her own life only a few months later. Stevie Smith had her *Selected Poems* published which included 1957's *Not Waving but Drowning* and St. Lucian bard and later Nobel Prize winner Derek Walcott produced *In a Green Night: Poems 1948-60*.

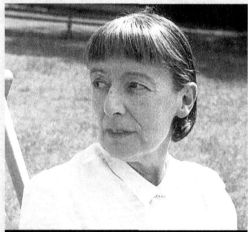
Poet Florence Margaret "Stevie" Smith

Comic book art saw the introduction of both *Spider-Man* and *The Incredible Hulk*. Both were victims of exposure to radiation which gave them superpowers. Andy Warhol's first one-man gallery exhibition opened at the Ferus Gallery in Los Angeles in July 1962. He exhibited his silk screen printed *Campbell's Soup Cans* work. It was an instant hit. It was the debut for pop art on the West Coast of America. In London the Queen's Gallery opened at Buckingham Palace. Before the millennium it would welcome over five million visitors to view works by artists such as Da Vinci, Titian, Rembrandt and Gainsborough.

Artist Andy Warhol

A Clockwork Orange

Author: Anthony Burgess   First published in 1962

A Clockwork Orange is one of those books which most people have heard of but which few have actually read. This is probably because it is preceded by a reputation of shocking ultra-violence. It features lengthy descriptions of heinous crimes. They are vivid descriptions, filled with chaos. Burgess later wrote in his autobiography: 'I was sickened by my own excitement at setting it down.' Yet it does not glorify violence, nor is it a book about violence per se. Rather it is an exploration of the morality of free will, of whether it is better to choose to be bad than to be conditioned to be good. It also describes alienation and how to deal with the excesses to which such alienation may lead. And ultimately it is about one man's decision to say goodbye to all that.

Two versions of the book were published. One with an upbeat ending, the other a far darker conclusion. When Stanley Kubrick adapted the book for cinema, he chose the darker ending.

One Flew Over the Cuckoo's Nest

Author: Ken Kesey   Published: February 1st 1962

Tyrannical Nurse Ratched rules over her ward in an Oregon State mental hospital with a strict and unbending routine. She is unopposed by her patients who are stupefied by mind-numbing medication and browbeaten by the threat of electric shock therapy. But her regime is disrupted by the arrival of McMurphy, a swaggering, mischievous trickster with a devilish grin. He resolves to oppose her rules on behalf of himself and his fellow inmates. His struggle is seen through the eyes of Chief Bromden, a seemingly mute half-Native American patient, who understands McMurphy's heroic attempt to do battle with the powers that keep them all imprisoned. Kesey's extraordinary debut novel is an exuberant, coarse and devastatingly honest portrayal of the boundary between sanity and madness. When a film was made of the book in 1975, Jack Nicholson played McMurphy as if the role had been specially written for him.

One Day in the Life of Ivan Denisovich

Author: Aleksandr Solzhenitsyn   First published in 1962

The novel is set in Stalinist Russia during the 1950s. It follows the suffering of a prisoner, Ivan Denisovich Shukhov, from the moment he is woken up at 5am to when he finally goes to bed after a day of back-breaking hard labour. Shukhov has been sentenced for a crime he did not commit. Whilst fighting for Russia in the Second World War, he was captured and imprisoned by the Germans. He managed to escape and return to his own lines, but was then accused of being a spy. He was given a choice: face a firing squad or sign a confession and go to a Gulag (prison camp) for ten years. On the day the book is set, Shukhov is already eight years into a ten-year sentence and is well used to the brutality of the guards, the freezing cold winters and the lack of food. This loosely autobiographical book was given special mention when Solzhenitsyn was awarded the Nobel Prize in literature in 1970.

Another Country

Author: James Baldwin   First published in 1962

Sprawling and introspective, *Another Country* explores the many forms love and longing can take. Set in Greenwich Village and Harlem during the late fifties, Baldwin's third novel centres on the malaise and messy affairs of a small group of friends following the grisly suicide of one of the circle's key members. Characters cheat on each other, cross class and racial boundaries and strive for greatness even as despair threatens to consume them. Again and again they ask themselves and others whether or not they are loved. The question is recited like an incantation throughout the novel's three slow-moving sections. With great insight Baldwin muses on the impact of social identity on romance. The book is best summed up in the passage - "People don't have any mercy. They tear you limb from limb, in the name of love. Then, when you're dead, when they've killed you by what they made you go through, they say you didn't have any character. They weep big, bitter tears- not for you. for themselves, because they've lost their toy."

The Golden Notebook

Author: Doris Lessing   First published in 1962

The Golden Notebook is a semi-autobiographical, labyrinthine novel by the Nobel Prize winning author Doris Lessing. The story revolves around a writer, Anna Wulf, the four notebooks in which she records her life and her attempts to tie them together in a fifth, gold coloured notebook. The

book intersperses segments of narrative of the lives of Anna and her friend, Molly Jacobs, as well as their children, ex-husbands and lovers, with excerpts from Anna's four notebooks. The notebook coloured black tells of Anna's experience of living in Southern Rhodesia before and during World War II. The red book relates to her time as a member of the Communist Party. Yellow is based on the painful ending of a love affair and blue is a personal journal where she records her memories, hopes and dreams. The book is non-chronological with each section overlapping until it is all pulled together by the emergence of the golden notebook.

Dead Cert

Author: Dick Francis   First published in 1962

Dick Francis' path into writing was a most unorthodox one. Riding the Queen Mother's horse, Devon Lock, in the 1956 Grand National, he fell off on the run to the line. Shortly afterwards Francis was advised to retire which is when he took up writing. With his inside knowledge of the racing game he wrote one novel a year until his death in 2020. In this, his first novel, he writes about crooked jockeys, bent bookmakers, gangsters muscling in on racing and suspected murder. It was also ironic that having been involved in an infamous Grand National moment, he would go on to play a big part in saving the race decades later. In 1983 the race stood on the verge of economic bankruptcy. Francis, along with other philanthropists, launched a global campaign to raise money to secure its future. Gamblers may tell you that there is no such thing as a dead cert; Francis, after accruing a fortune from writing, might have disagreed.

Dr. Seuss' Sleep Book
Written and illustrated by Theodor Seuss Geisel (aka Dr. Seuss)

Literary history is littered with books that, though started, were almost impossible to finish. Tolstoy's *War and Peace* and Joyce's *Ulysses* spring to mind. However, few books are specifically designed not to be finished. *Dr. Seuss' Sleep Book* is one such book. Written to be read by a parent to a young child or by the child when slightly older, the book has a magical sleep-inducing effect. It is full of rhyming couplets illustrated by weird and wonderful characters all dressed for bed. "A yawn is quite catching, you see, like a cough. It just takes one yawn to start other yawns off." It is stated that a single yawn can set off a chain reaction which causes "ninety-nine zillion nine trillion and two" creatures to sleep. The last line of the book reads simply "good night", but if the narrator has got that far they probably know that they are in trouble. It stands as one of the most popular children's books ever written and is regularly passed on from generation to generation.

The Wolves of Willoughby Chase
Author: Joan Aikin   First published in 1962

The book is a fantasy novel aimed at pre-teen children. It is nominally set in 1832, but in reality it occupies a world that does not exist. For example there is a passage where England is invaded by wolves who travel through a channel tunnel. It starts when shy Sylvia goes to live with her cousin Bonnie, daughter of the rich owners of Willoughby Chase. When Bonnie's parents leave for a trip overseas, the girls are left under the guardianship of the cruel Miss Slighcarp. Almost immediately the girls realise that something is wrong. Miss Slighcarp locks Bonnie in a wardrobe for being naughty and then sacks all but an untrustworthy few of the household staff. Things are to get worse as the evil governess sells all of Bonnie's toys as well as anything else that is not fixed to the ground. She then packs the girls off to a boarding school that is run by some unscrupulous friends, which is more akin to a prison. The girls vow to escape and save Willoughby Chase. With the aid of some weird and wonderful characters on the way, they triumph in the end.

Tales from Moominvalley (The Moomins #7)
Author and illustrator: Tove Jannson   First published in English in 1962

Jansson was an artist, writer and satirist. Her most famous creation was the Moomins, where she drew heavily on her bohemian upbringing in Finland. Her first language was Swedish and the directness of the language translated well into English, giving her stories added power. Unlike the majority of the Moomins books which tell a single story, this is a collection of very small tales (mostly about creatures with very small tails). The stories all centre around them not fitting in with society. Usually they want to get away from others and be left in peace, or they want rid of their worldly possessions that are weighing them down. Often they find great contentment through the love of others when you are kind. But mostly, the little creatures are just pleased to be free of boredom and burden. The funniest perhaps is the last one: *The Fir Tree*, in which the Moomins, who normally hibernate, are woken up for Christmas and try to make sense of it.

Paul Scofield

King Lear

Written by William Shakespeare
Directed by Peter Brook with Paul Scofield as King Lear
Premiered on 11th September 1962 at the Royal Shakespeare Theatre

Ever since it was written in around 1606, William Shakespeare's *King Lear* had almost universally portrayed the King as a felled giant driven mad by his three scheming daughters, Regan, Goneril and Cordelia. Peter Brook, probably the greatest British theatre director, reworked the play. In his production he presented Lear as an edgy, volatile character who was difficult to live with. The result was revolutionary. Instead of assuming that Lear was right, the audience was asked to examine the motives of all the protagonists from a standpoint of moral neutrality.

Eventually spurned by his daughters, Lear loses his wits solely to punish them. He announces "I fear I am not of perfect mind." The Observer theatre critic Kenneth Tynan proclaimed the production to be the greatest he had seen, writing: "This production brings me closer to Lear than I have ever been; from now on, I not only know him but can place him in his harsh and unforgiving world." Brook went on to direct many of the greatest actors of the day in Shakespearean productions, including Glenda Jackson as Cleopatra, Ben Kingsley as Demetrius and Patrick Stewart as Snout.

Uta Hagen

Who's Afraid of Virginia Woolf?

Written by Edward Albee
Starring Uta Hagen, Arthur Hill and Ben Piazza
First performance: Billy Rose Theatre, New York October 13th 1962

The most enduring play of 1962, *Who's Afraid of Virginia Woolf?* was met with huge public and critical acclaim. The three act play begins with an argument between Martha and her husband, history professor George. Unbeknownst to George, Martha has invited young biology professor Nick and his wife Honey over for drinks. Drinking held Martha and George's marriage together, but it also laid bare the dysfunctional nature of their relationship. The first act, entitled *Fun and Games*, is painful to watch. Act II, *Walpurgistnacht*, sees the two men in deep conversation while the ladies leave the stage. Upon their return, they enter into a game of "humiliate the host". The tension mounts and by Act III, *The Exorcism*, the horrible truth of what brings these two couples together is finally revealed. The play was brought to a wider audience when Elizabeth Taylor and Richard Burton, then husband and wife, starred in a film version in 1966 with a supporting cast of George Segal and Sandy Dennis. It won Taylor both a BAFTA and an Academy Award for best actress. Burton scooped a BAFTA for best actor, but failed at the Oscars - one of seven nominations without success throughout his career. Albee used the royalties from the play to set up a foundation to help young writers and artists. Among those to benefit were Spalding Gray and Sean Scully.

John Masefield, Poet Laureate (served 1930-1967)

John Masefield

Masefield was the longest serving Poet Laureate to serve entirely within the 20th century. His 37 years of service was only beaten by Alfred, Lord Tennyson who held the post between 1850-1892. By the 1950s Masefield seemed from a bygone era as traditional poetry had fallen out of public favour, whilst more modernist poets such as Sylvia Plath and Stevie Smith were gaining more traction. The emerging Beat Generation of poets such as Ginsburg, Carr and Huncke seemed to speak more to the youth of the day than did the rather staid Masefield. Still, he took his job seriously and acted as all good Poets Laureate do and wrote poems for the court, in his case the House of Windsor. Rather quaintly, Masefield would send his poems to the Times of London for their approval with a stamped addressed envelope for their response. Even though he seemed more like a 19th century poet than most of his contemporaries, many of his poems still stand the test of time. His *Sonnets and Poems* written in the midst of World War I and *A Generation Risen* written during World War II defined him as a chronicler of British 20th century history. He is one of the few poets to have written during both wars. In 1961 he published his collection *The Bluebells and Other Verses*, which was one of the best selling poetry books of 1962.

The Role of Poet Laureate Through The Ages

The monarch of the day bestows the honorary position of Poet Laureate, currently on the advice of the prime minister. There are no specific duties to the role, although it is expected that the holder produces original verse to commemorate significant national occasions. The first official Poet Laureate was John Dryden who was appointed by Charles II in 1668. Until Andrew Motion was appointed in 1999 the laureateship was held for life; subsequently the position has been offered for a fixed term of 10 years. Other notable Poets Laureate included William Wordsworth (1843-1850), Sir John Betjeman (1972-1984) and Ted Hughes (1984-1998). The actor Daniel Day-Lewis's father, Cecil, was also Poet Laureate from 1968 to 1972. It was only in 2009 that the first woman, Carol Ann Duffy, was offered the role. She was also the first Scot.

Sir John Betjeman

Carol Ann Duffy

The role of Poet Laureate is not a money spinner; Andrew Motion and Carol Ann Duffy were offered annual salaries of £5,750 per year. However, in a quirky tradition dating back to Charles I, the holder also receives a barrel of sherry.

Atlas - One of the World's First Supercomputers

The Atlas machine in Manchester

During the 1950s the race to design and build ever more powerful computers was intense. Academic institutions had seen the potential for these machines to be hired out to commercial organisations to run programs that solved complex mathematical problems. In 1956 the Brunt committee reported to the government that Britain was falling behind the US in computer development. This report seeded the idea for what would become the Atlas supercomputer, though it wasn't until 1959 that the funding was in place. Through a joint venture between the University of Manchester, Ferranti International and Plessey, the first ever Atlas machine went into operation in 1962 at the university. It was said that when it was not in use, half of the UK's total computer capacity was lost. It was the first computer to use virtual memory which is now ubiquitous. Two other machines were subsequently built: one in Cambridge and the other for the Atomic Weapons Research Establishment in Aldermaston. The University of Manchester would charge customers £500 per hour to use the machine; by 1969 it had generated an estimated £720,000 in revenue. The Manchester Atlas was highly regarded in the industry and would go on to complete 10 years of service.

J.C.R Licklider - The Internet Pioneer

Joseph Carl Robnett Licklider

Joseph Carl Robnett Licklider was a computer scientist and psychologist who is considered to be one of the most influential figures and visionaries in computer science development. Long before they were developed he foresaw graphical computing, point-and-click interfaces, digital libraries, e-commerce, online banking and, most profoundly, the internet itself.

He was born in St.Louis, Missouri in 1915 and excelled throughout his education gaining a triple major in Physics, Mathematics and Psychology in 1937 before becoming a research fellow at Harvard University in the 1940s. In 1960 his seminal paper "Man-Computer Symbiosis" predicted the rise of interactive computing. He conceived, funded and managed research that led to modern personal computers. He is also credited as being a pioneer in artificial intelligence (AI) and cybernetics. In a series of memos in 1962 he discussed the "Intergalactic Computer Network" concept. Within these memos are nearly all the elements of what we know as the internet today including the development of cloud computing.

Spacewar! - One of the World's First Video Games

Spacewar! was developed in 1962 by American computer scientist Steve Russell. It was written for the DEC PDP-1 minicomputer which had been recently installed at the Massachusetts Institute of Technology (MIT). The two-player game features two spaceships named "the needle" and "the wedge" locked in a dogfight in the gravity well of a star. The aim is to destroy the opponent's ship by torpedoing them or making them crash

Control panel of the PDP-1

Spacewar! on the PDP-1 screen

into the star. Initially buttons were used to control the ships until Bob Saunders designed an early gamepad to make it easier to play. Although PDP-1 computers cost the equivalent of $1million, the game was installed in multiple machines making it the first video game ever to be played at multiple computer installations. It would go on to inspire video game designers for generations to come. It directly influenced the design of the iconic *Asteroids* arcade game which was launched in 1979.

In 2007 it was listed in the ten most important video games of all time thereby entering the 'Game Canon' register stored at the US Library of Congress which lists games worthy of preservation. In 2018 it was entered into the World Video Game Hall of Fame.

The Creation of the Compact Audio Cassette Tape

The Compact Audio Cassette

The origins of the audio cassette tape can be traced back to 1888 when American Oberlin Smith invented a method of recording sound by magnetising wire. This led to German Fritz Pfleumer inventing magnetic tape in 1928 which in turn led to the first reel-to-reel tape recorders appearing in 1935. However these machines were expensive and difficult to use, so were mostly found in radio stations and recording studios. It wasn't until 1962 when Lou Ottens and his team, working for Dutch company Phillips, invented a miniaturised version of magnetic tape. The concept of the compact audio cassette tape was born. It was commercially introduced a year later at the Berlin Radio Show and would go on to revolutionise how we listen to music. The ability to both take your music with you and also record your own 'mix tapes' caught the public's imagination. Although the development team initially envisaged the use of cassettes for dictation, the quality of the audio was such that its use for music quickly dominated. Sony turbocharged the demand for audio cassettes in 1979 when it released the first ever Walkman. The 3.81mm wide tape typically was made of polyester with a coating of metal oxide such as Ferric Oxide which was magnetised to encode the recording. Two stereo pairs of tracks were available; one when the cassette was played in one direction and the other when the cassette was flipped, or in subsequent years, when an auto-reverse mechanism was actuated.

Telstar-1

The Telstar-1 satellite

On 10th July 1962 a Thor-Delta rocket blasted off from Cape Canaveral carrying on-board Telstar-1 in the first ever privately sponsored space launch. Belonging to AT&T, Telstar was part of a multi-national agreement between Bell Telephone Laboratories, NASA, The General Post Office in the UK and National PTT in France to develop an experimental satellite communications systems over the Atlantic. Telstar-1 was deployed in an elliptical orbit around the earth which it would complete every 2 hours and 37 minutes. During its orbit it would travel to its furthest point from the Earth (the apogee) some 3,687 miles away, whilst its perigee (point closest to Earth) was 592 miles above the planet. Due to this elliptical path, transatlantic satellite signals were only available for 30 minutes every orbit. Since the transmitters and receivers on the satellite were not very powerful, enormous ground antennae had to be built on both sides of the Atlantic. The first non-public television pictures were relayed the day after launch. However, it would be two weeks later on 23rd July that the first live transatlantic broadcast took place featuring TV presenters including Richard Dimbleby and Walter Cronkite. The broadcast also featured a speech by President Kennedy.

John Glenn Orbits The Earth

John Glenn on-board Friendship 7

In the space race between the Americans and the Russians, it was Russia who were first to successfully complete a manned orbital mission around the Earth. On April 12th 1961 Yuri Gagarin flew his Vostok spacecraft one complete orbit of the earth in a mission that lasted 108 minutes from launch to landing. A few months later, the Vostok 2 mission managed 17 orbits of the earth in a prolonged flight. It took the Americans a further 6 months to launch their first orbital mission. NASA had hoped to launch in late 1961 to match the Russians, but delays in the hardware scuppered those plans. On February 20th 1962 American astronaut John Glenn took off from Cape Canaveral on-board his spacecraft Friendship 7, as part of NASA's Project Mercury. He orbited the earth 3 times in the flight making many notable observations including spotting a dust storm in Nigeria and seeing a very bright light in Australia, which turned out to be the city of Perth whose residents had switched on all their lights for the fly past. Glenn successfully touched down in his capsule in the Atlantic ocean and was picked up 17 minutes later by USS Noa. He returned to the United States a hero.

Mariner 2

An artist's impression of the Mariner 2 probe set against a real photo of Venus

Mariner 2 was an American space probe, the first in history to successfully encounter another planet. The planet in question was Venus, the second closest planet to the sun. Mariner 2 was launched in August 1962, just over a month after the Mariner 1 mission had ended in failure. Back in July, Mariner 1 had started to veer off course soon after liftoff so had to be destroyed. It turned out this was caused by the omission of a hyphen symbol in the guidance program. Science-fiction author Arthur C. Clarke called the error "the most expensive hyphen in history". However the Mariner 2 mission had no such problems. On December 14th 1962 the probe passed as close as 21,607 miles from the surface of Venus, taking a number of measurements with its on-board sensors. Originally the Mariner probes had more instrumentation on-board including a TV camera, but these had to be removed to save weight. The original, larger launch rocket had to be replaced with a smaller rocket which was more limited in its payload capacity. However, Mariner 2 was able to report that Venus has cool clouds in its atmosphere but its surface is a scorching 500 degrees C.

3C 273 - The First Quasar To Be Identified

3C 273 photo from The Hubble telescope

The word quasar is a contraction of the expression quasi-stellar radio source. They were so named as they looked star-like to astronomers who first noticed them in the late 1950s. 3C refers to the Third Cambridge Catalogue of Radio Sources published in 1959 with this being the 273rd object identified. It was observations carried out by British astronomer, Cyril Hazard, on August 5th 1962 which led to the declaration that this bright object was indeed a Quasar. Scientists now know that Quasars are not stars, they are young galaxies located vast distances from the earth. They increase in number towards the edge of the visible universe. 3C 273 is several billion light years away from Earth meaning that the light we see comes from a time when our universe was much younger. The oldest Quasar so far detected is 13 billion light years away meaning we are seeing its light only 670 million years after the Big Bang. 3C 273 is hundreds of times brighter than our own Milky Way and is visible in the northern and southern hemispheres every May. It is the most distant celestial object that average amateur astronomers are likely to see through their telescopes.

The First Successful Whole Hip Replacement Operation

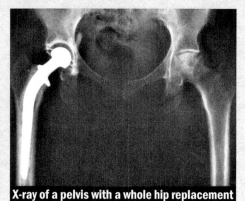
X-ray of a pelvis with a whole hip replacement

Sir John Charnley was born in 1911 in Lancashire. His dad was a chemist and his mother a nurse. Through school he showed an aptitude for science leading him to study medicine at the University of Manchester. His medical career was interrupted by World War II when he joined the Royal Army Medical Corps. Charnley participated in the British evacuation of Dunkirk. Later he was posted to Cairo, where he spent the rest of the war under the supervision of orthopaedic surgeon Dudley Buxton. Charnley's pioneering career in orthopaedic surgery had begun. He returned to Manchester after the war eventually raising funding to open a specialised hip surgery centre at the Wrightington Hospital in Lancashire. Charnley's experimentation with new materials for artificial hips was not always successful. In 1960 he performed experimental operations involving PTFE coated joints which, at first, appeared to be a success. However, after a year the joints showed signs of wear requiring a second operation to have them removed. His determination was unwavering which led to his discovery of High Molecular Weight Polyethylene (HMWP) as an alternative to PTFE. In November 1962 he performed the first whole hip replacement using HMWP. After 5 years careful observation of his patients, he hailed the operations a success. He was knighted for his service to medicine in 1977.

Propranolol - The World's First Beta Blocker

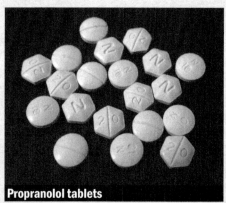
Propranolol tablets

James Whyte Black was a quiet, unassuming Scotsman who would who go on to become one of the greatest scientists of the modern age. He was born the fourth of five sons to a Baptist family in Lanarkshire, Scotland in 1924. Gifted as a child, he was persuaded by his maths teacher to sit the entrance exam to St. Andrew's University whilst still only 15-years-old. His family were too poor to send him to university, but he won a scholarship which enabled him to study medicine there. After university he took a teaching job in Singapore for three years to help pay off his not insubstantial debts. Returning to the UK in the early 1950s he developed an interest in the way adrenaline affects the human heart, especially for those with angina. He formulated a theory as to how the effects of adrenaline could be counteracted. He joined ICI Pharmaceuticals in 1958, and it was whilst working there in 1962 he invented and patented Propranolol, the world's first Beta Blocker. It would go on to become the world's best-selling drug. It was hailed as the greatest breakthrough in the treatment of heart disease since the discovery of Digitalis (from Foxgloves) in the 18th century. Black was a private man but he was awarded multiple public honours for his work. These included a knighthood in 1981 followed by appointment to the Order of Merit in 2000, of which there are only ever 24 members at any one time.

The Century 21 Exposition aka Seattle World's Fair

World Fairs have a long history dating back to the 18th century when the first one was held in Prague in 1791. They are designed to showcase the achievements of nations. Notable world fairs have included the 1851 Great Exhibition in London and the 1889 World's Fair in Paris, which gave us the Eiffel Tower. As the home of Boeing and other technological businesses, the city of Seattle pushed to stage a World Fair in 1962 to showcase the USA's modern science, space exploration and progressive future thinking. It started as the brainchild of City Councilman Al Rochester back in 1955. He worked tirelessly over many years to convince decision makers, financial backers and the public to get behind the project. A 28-acre parcel of land in the city was chosen as the site which would see a series of exhibition centres and auditoriums built to accommodate the incredibly diverse exhibitions from the USA and 35 other nation states. The centrepiece was a stunning observation tower standing at 605 ft (184m) tall dubbed 'The Space Needle'. Built to withstand 200mph winds and a 9.0 magnitude earthquake, the Space Needle has become an icon of the city. Amidst 538

The Space Needle Tower

clanging bells, 2000 balloons and 10 Air Force fighters flying overhead, the Century 21 Exposition opened its doors to the public on April 21st 1962. It would eventually welcome nearly 10 million visitors in the six months it was open. The grounds of the fair were divided into many zones including the World of Science, the World of Tomorrow, the World of Commerce and Industry, the World of Art and the World of Entertainment. Many commercial sponsors took part to showcase their latest and future products including Pan-Am, General Motors, Bell Telephone and Boeing. The World of Science featured the Spacearium which took visitors on a simulated voyage

GM displayed its Firebird III prototype

through the Solar System, the Milky Way and beyond. Also in the World of Science visitors rode 'The Bubbleator' which took them on a ride into the future accompanied by music and lights. In the World of Entertainment many world famous artists performed during the fair. The opening night at the Opera House saw a performance by the Seattle Symphony Orchestra with guest conductor Igor Stravinsky, one of the most influential composers of the 20th century. To transport people to the fair, the Alweg Monorail was constructed in just 8 months at a cost of $4.2 million. The two trains each carry 450 people along a 0.9 mile track with the trip taking two minutes. The monorail still runs to this day. Overall the Century 21 Exposition was both a financial and critical success.

The Alweg Monorail built for the fair

Days from Nuclear War | October 16ᵗʰ to 29ᵗʰ

Far from being a little local difficulty in the Caribbean, what became known as the Cuban Missile Crisis came dangerously close to triggering all out nuclear war between the two superpowers of the day, America and the Soviet Union. Both nations had enough firepower to wipe out most of the northern hemisphere. When Fidel Castro led a guerrilla army that overthrew the Batista regime in 1959, he reached out to America for recognition. In 1961 America responded by sponsoring an invasion by mainly Floridian Cuban exiles at the Bay of Pigs. This was easily fought off by Castro's heavily armed and disciplined forces. The result of

JFK meeting with his military generals

America's actions was to push the new Cuban regime further into the hands of Communist Russia. In the knowledge that the Soviets were eager to provide economic and military support to prop up fellow communist regimes, the Kennedy administration remained watchful of the Kremlin's relationship with Castro. In 1962, tensions grew as American spy planes provided clear evidence that Soviet nuclear missiles were being shipped to Cuba. The fact that the ballistic missiles could reach America's eastern seaboard

US Navy plane flies over a Soviet ship carrying missiles

within minutes greatly concerned the White House. With the memory of World War II fresh in the mind, President John F. Kennedy warned the US public that they might once again have to pay "the price for freedom" as conflict, this time with Russia, could not be ruled out. Washington's hawkish stance did not receive immediate backing from their allies. Britain, still smarting from America's lukewarm response to the Suez Crisis of 1956, did eventually offer support but much of Western Europe simply held their breath. The proximity to Russia and the threat of nuclear annihilation meant that Kennedy's brinkmanship was not to their liking. Kennedy, who had initially planned a full-scale invasion of Cuba,

Potential range of Russian missiles

decided instead to mount a naval blockade. He also called upon his Soviet counterpart, Nikita Khrushchev, to "halt and eliminate this clandestine, reckless and provocative threat to world peace". In an unbearably tense showdown, a fleet of Russian ships bound for Cuba held its course despite threats of attack from America. As the ships edged closer to the Cuban coastline they received instructions from Moscow to turn back, thus averting confrontation with the US navy. Days later, the deadly game of risk between the two superpowers ended. Khrushchev sent Kennedy a message that Russian missiles would be removed from Cuba and, in return, Kennedy vowed that the US would never invade Cuba. The people of the world, who for two weeks had gone to bed not knowing if there would be a tomorrow, breathed a collective sigh of relief. "Khrushchev blinked", ran the headlines in the Western media, but in truth Kennedy blinked as well. America had secretly been stockpiling missiles on Russia's doorstep in Turkey and, as part of a secret deal, they agreed to remove them.

The Winter of 1962/63

The Big Freeze of 1962-63 was one of the coldest winters on record in the UK. When we look at the Central England Temperature records, which extend back to 1659, only the winters of 1683-84 and 1739-40 have been colder. The most severe conditions were across England and Wales. Although winter hit hard in Scotland, it didn't rank as one of its worst on record. The temperatures plummeted for weeks on end causing rivers, lakes and even the sea to freeze over. The first few weeks of December 1962 had been changeable and stormy, but then on 22nd December there was a sudden change in the weather as high pressure moved to the north-east of the UK dragging bitingly cold winds across the country. Once this weather pattern had set in, it did not change much

Telephone wires collapsed under the ice

for the rest of the winter. On 24th December a weather front moved south across the UK turning to snow as it did so. Glasgow had its first white Christmas since 1938. The snow reached southern England on Boxing Day with some places seeing falls of up to 12 inches. A blizzard on 29th and 30th December hit Wales and the south west of England causing snowdrifts up to 20ft deep. Widespread disruption followed as many roads and railways were blocked and telephone lines brought down leaving some villages left cut off for several days. Poole Harbour froze over, as did a section of the Thames in Berkshire. The snow was so deep that farmers couldn't get to their livestock causing many animals to perish. On Dartmoor, 6,000 animals went without food for 4 days until helicopters could drop in supplies. The effect on wildlife was also severe. The New Forest's Dartford warbler

Deep snow in Lancashire

population was almost wiped out. Garden birds such as the wren and the goldcrest saw their numbers greatly depleted. This snow set the scene for the next two and a half months, as much of England remained covered every day until early March 1963. Blizzards, snowdrifts and blocks of ice were commonplace with temperatures dropping below -20°C, colder than the winter of 1947 and the coldest since 1740. In Braemar, Scotland, the temperature plummeted to -22.2°C on 18th January. Sport suffered greatly and the 3rd round of the F.A. Cup took 66 days to complete. Manchester City went 70 days without playing a match. When football could be played it took place on icy pitches. On 26th December 1962, Brian Clough suffered a career ending injury

Clearing this drive took all day

caused by a slippery pitch. Although he made a short-lived comeback two years later, he then retired and became the greatest manager of his generation. The thaw didn't truly begin until the beginning of March 1963 when mild, south westerly winds led to an increase in the temperature. By 6th March, there were no frosts anywhere in the UK and the temperature in London reached 17°C. The snow quickly melted and with the thaw came flooding, though thankfully none of it was major.

Havoc from Sheffield to Hamburg

On February 16th a huge storm hit Yorkshire, centring around the city of Sheffield. It had formed over the North Atlantic some two days earlier. It caused extensive damage to the city and surrounding areas leaving nine people dead in its wake. What became known as the Great Sheffield Gale was made worse by the unique topography of the region. Winds were funnelled through the valleys of the River Don and River

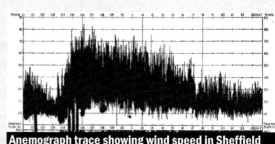
Anemograph trace showing wind speed in Sheffield

Sheaf reaching hurricane force at times. The huge storm was not only confined to Yorkshire. Winds of 177mph were recorded in North Uist, Shetland. (Shetland holds the record for wind speed in the UK, when winds reached 197mph during the New Year's Day storm of 1992.) Storm Vincinette then gathered intensity in the North Sea and wreaked havoc on the North German city of Hamburg. The city had been virtually destroyed some 19 years earlier by Allied bombing raids during World War II. In the rebuilding of the city, flood defences were not considered a high priority, but no-one could have foreseen the catastrophic weather event that was about to strike. Overnight on the 16th/17th February a

Submerged cars in the streets of Hamburg

devastating flood spilled over the north German coast. The storm front pushed gargantuan amounts of water into the mouth of the River Elbe, thrusting a flood wave 19-feet high towards the city's flood protection system. At around midnight, when most residents were asleep, the Elbe broke through the city's dyke system at over 60 locations resulting in nearly one fifth of the municipal area being submerged. The southern parts of the city were worst affected. This included the densely populated borough of Wilhelmsburg, whose inhabitants suffered the most. This unexpected flood caused the entire region's infrastructure to collapse forcing surviving residents to be trapped in their homes. Hamburg's minister of the interior, and future German Chancellor, Helmut Schmidt, launched an unprecedented rescue operation, calling on the German army, the Red Cross, the fire department and NATO forces who were still stationed in Germany. Over 25,000 aid workers entered the disaster area aided by lifeboats and helicopters. More than 10,000 people

The River Elbe burst its banks

were successfully rescued, but sadly 315 died in Hamburg and a further 35 lost their lives across the region. Countless farm animals and pets also perished. The shock surrounding the flood and the fragility of security measures led to a turning point in coastal protection and disaster preparedness that resonates today. These included the planning and construction of new flood protection installations, increasing the height and robustness of the old dykes, and the establishment of a contingency plan for future disasters. Hamburg has suffered a number of similar weather events, notably in 1976, 1982 and 2007, but no comparable disaster has struck the North Sea coast since 1962.

Night of the Long Knives

When Harold Macmillan took over the reigns of power from Anthony Eden in 1957, he seemed a breath of fresh air. Eden had badly handled the Suez Crisis of 1956 whilst Macmillan painted himself as a man who could take postcolonial Britain forward. In 1960 he spent a month in Africa concluding that the "Winds of change were blowing over the continent." He was also on top of domestic policy, declaring that "You will see a state of prosperity as we have never had in my lifetime, nor indeed in the history of our country." The press quickly paraphrased this as "You've never had it so good." The boom times of the late 1950s quickly turned to bust. Inflation began to take hold and productivity declined. Equally important was the fact that "Supermac", as he was portrayed, was increasingly looking like a man out of time. Born in the 19th century and injured in the Great War, he seemed aloof and dated. Harold Wilson was soon to promise the "White heat of

Prime Minister Harold Macmillan

technology" while Macmillan seemed increasingly to look to the past. Local government elections had gone badly and by-elections, particularly in the safe seat of Orpington, even worse. The Chancellor Selwyn Lloyd's credit squeeze, where he raised interest rates, was unpopular with voters. The Cabinet was fractious and there were complaints of a lack of leadership. One Tory backbencher had broken cover to say the Prime Minister should go. For Harold Macmillan 1962 was not going well and he feared worse was to come. A colleague recalled Macmillan saying that there was a danger of a split in the Cabinet, implying a conspiracy against him. Why he reacted to this in the way he did is still a matter of debate. Perhaps he was panicked by the press or by concern for sterling, or perhaps the whole thing was done in cold blood. Either way, the event has assumed a place in history as Macmillan's 'Night of the Long Knives'. On Friday 13th July he announced that he was sacking seven Cabinet ministers, including the Chancellor of the Exchequer, Selwyn Lloyd, and the Lord Chancellor, Lord Kilmuir. This set in motion a wholesale government reshuffle which involved 52 people and affected 39 of the 101 ministerial posts. If the scale was breathtaking, so was the style. Dismissing senior colleagues with long years of loyal service behind them, Macmillan was graceless and brutal. Customary courtesies were omitted and the usual pretence that the parting was by mutual agreement was forgotten. Even those who had previously indicated they might be ready to move on were, as one said, 'exposed to the greatest possible degree of publicity and stress'. Nothing like it had ever been seen before in British politics. The Daily Telegraph gasped at the 'Stalinist scale of the purge' and the Conservative Party was reported to be 'pole-axed by shock'. Macmillan's actions have been portrayed as the ultimate display of a Prime Minister's power over their colleagues. In 1963 the Profumo scandal finally brought Macmillan down,

Selwyn Lloyd was one of those sacked

but the seeds had been sown in 1962.

The Coppenhall Junction Disaster

On the evening of 26th December 1962, bitingly cold weather and snow in and around the Cheshire town of Crewe caused points to freeze and trains to be halted at signals. Many people were on there way back from visiting relatives for the Yuletide festivities, others were on their way back from work. Midway between Winsford and Crewe was the Midday Scot, making its way from Glasgow Central station to London Euston with 500 people on-board. It ground to a halt at a red signal. The driver found the telephone to Coppenhall Junction, the next signal box ahead, out of order. As he was able to see the signal after that, he

Carriages telescoped into one another hampering rescue attempts

decided to proceed towards it and use the telephone there. In the darkness, the driver failed to notice the 16:45 express from Liverpool to Birmingham (with 8 coaches and 300 passengers) stationery on the line ahead. He collided with it at about 20 mph (32 km/h). The rear coaches of the Liverpool train were badly damaged in the collision, some of them being telescoped. 18 passengers were killed and 34 were badly injured. A great many other passengers received minor injuries and were treated on the spot in a massive and complex rescue effort.

The Netherlands' Worst Ever Railway Disaster

At the start of the year, Holland was to suffer its worst railway disaster. On January 8th two passenger trains collided head on at full speed at Harmelen, near Utrecht. Over 500 commuters were travelling to work during the early morning rush hour. Both drivers died in the crash. It is presumed that dense fog caused one of them not to see and obey a red signal. As well as the 2 drivers, 91 passengers lost their lives and scores more suffered serious injury. To this day it is the Netherlands' worst railway accident. After a lengthy investigation it was decided to

Aftermath of the disaster

introduce an automatic braking system which would prevent drivers passing a red light. The Automatische Trein Beinvloeding (ABT) was cutting edge technology for the time. It was a major leap forward in train safety which was adopted by several other countries.

The Trial of Adolph Eichmann

At the end of World War II, American forces captured Adolph Eichmann. However, he managed to escape from their prison camp in 1946. After assuming a false identity, he lived in occupied Germany for over a decade. Eventually he made his way to Argentina, via Austria and Italy and settled there in 1958. Unbeknownst to him, the Israeli Secret Service was hot on his tail. On May 11th they "arrested" him, then nine days later smuggled him out of the country and took him to Israel. The fact that this was against both Argentinian and International Law caused a diplomatic incident. However, the Israelis were prepared to ride out the storm. In their eyes they had captured one of the architects of the Holocaust and were going to put him on trial. The trial itself was controversial from the outset. Held before Jewish judges in a Jewish state that did not exist until three years after the Holocaust, gave rise to accusations that the trial was illegal. Many called for an

Adolph Eichmann in 1942

international court to try Eichmann while others even wanted him to be tried in Germany. Israel held firm. At stake was not only justice, but also the opportunity to educate a new generation about the Holocaust. During the trial, Eichmann did everything to try to save his own skin. In his defence he claimed not to be an anti-Semite. He claimed never to have read Hitler's diatribe *Mein Kampf* and, describing a previous visit to Haifa, he claimed he was more interested in the Jews than the Arabs. Incredibly, he also testified that he bought and read *Encyclopedia Judaica* and

Eichmann's three trial judges

Theodor Herzl's *The Jewish State*. Finally, he claimed to be a mere pawn in a game and was a low-ranking official simply following orders. In truth, he was one of the chief architects of the Holocaust as an attendee of the Wannsee Conference of 1942. His trial lasted from April 11th to December 15th 1961. Eichmann was sentenced to death, the only death sentence ever imposed by an Israeli court. Eichmann was hanged at around midnight on May 31st 1962; his ashes scattered at sea, so that there would be no permanent memorial.

Eichmann in the dock

In the yard of Ayalon Prison

The Ranrahirca Avalanche

Mount Huascarán rises 22,000 feet (approx. 6,000m) above sea level in the heart of the Andes mountain chain. Beneath it lay many Peruvian villages, whose inhabitants farmed in the fertile Rio Santa Valley. On the evening of January 10th, as most of the region's people gathered in their homes for dinner, the edge of a huge glacier suddenly broke apart and thundered down the mountain. The block of ice was the size of two aircraft carriers and weighed approximately six million tonnes. It made a terrifying noise as it fell, which was heard in the

Mount Huascarán in the Peruvian province of Yungay

towns below. As avalanches were not unusual in the area, it was embedded within folk law that there was usually a 20 to 30 minute gap between the sound of the ice cracking off and an avalanche arrive. This normally would have given people a window of opportunity to escape to higher ground. However, this time the avalanche travelled nine-and-a-half miles in only seven minutes, wiping away several communities. The towns of Ranrahirca and Huarascucho were buried under 40 feet of ice, mud, trees, boulders and other debris. Relief efforts were hampered by the very storm that sparked

The avalanche roared down at 77mph

off the avalanche. Colonel Umberto Ampuera, who led rescue attempts, described the area as being "like a scene from Dante's Inferno." Two Peruvian Air Force planes were dispatched to provide relief supplies whilst the army were sent to open up roads. Tragically, there were few people left to help. Only a handful of people in each town survived. The avalanche finally stopped at the Santa River, blocking it and causing flooding in nearby areas. Overall,

Remains of Yungay's cathedral after the 1970 avalanche

approximately 4,000 people lost their lives in the disaster. Some bodies were carried all the way to the Pacific Ocean near Chimbote, over 60 miles away. Others were buried under so much debris that their bodies were never recovered. Over 10,000 farm animals were killed and millions of dollars worth of crops were destroyed. The tragedy was compounded by the actions of the local government. In the September of that year, the Massachusetts Institute of Technology sponsored an expedition to examine surrounding glaciers. Two climbers, David Bernays and Charles Sawyer, found that in the aftermath of the avalanche a massive vertical slab of rock was being undermined by the glacier. Although their findings were published, the authorities ordered them to be retracted. They even threatened the climbers and anyone who repeated their research with imprisonment. The climbers fled back to America. On May 31st 1970 an even more deadly avalanche happened on the same mountain, this time killing over 30,000 people. That event remains the deadliest avalanche or glacier related disaster in history. The village of Ranrahirca no longer exists.

The Seaham Lifeboat Disaster

Britain, as a series of islands, owes a great debt to the men and women volunteers of the Royal National Lifeboat Institute who put the lives of others before their own. On call for large periods of time, they often sacrifice their social life in addition to holding down a regular job. At 3.55pm on the afternoon of 17th November, Captain R. Hudson, the secretary of the Seaham lifeboat station, received a call from the coastguard. According to a report from a local fisherman, a small boat was still at sea despite weather conditions rapidly deteriorating. Hudson immediately gave orders for the lifeboat assembly signal to be made. Flares, known as maroons, were fired at four o'clock. Soon after the Seaham lifeboat, George Elmy, was launched. She was a 35-foot Liverpool Class boat and on that day had a crew of five aboard. They were: Coxswain

Artist's impression of heavy seas battering the Seaham harbour walls

John T. Miller, Second Coxswain Fred Gippert, Bowman James Farrington, mechanic Leonard Brown, and Arthur Brown. When the lifeboat left the harbour, a north-by-east wind of force 6 was blowing; this rapidly increased to force 8 with gusts of storm force 10. There was a rough sea with an unpredictable swell, and the weather was overcast with blustery showers. Visibility was about two to three miles. It was two hours before high water, and the tide was setting south-by-west at a rate of over ten knots. As twenty-foot waves started to lash the harbour walls, the crew managed to reach the fishing vessel. Coxswain Miller had to bring the lifeboat alongside multiple times before

The George Elmy was discovered upturned the next morning (credit: East Durham Heritage & Lifeboat Centre)

the crew of five could be taken off the fishing vessel. At just before 5pm the lifeboat reported that she had the crew of the fishing vessel on-board. The lifeboat was making good headway back to the harbour when her lights were temporarily obscured by the drum end of the south pier. Standing on the pier Captain Hudson and a pilot, Captain Tait, spotted the lifeboat in difficulty as the George Elmy's red port light and green starboard light seemed to spin around in a circular direction. Thirty feet from the pier and agonisingly close to the entrance to the harbour, the lifeboat was seen to capsize. The time was 5.15pm. Only one man survived the tragedy. Donald Burrell, who had been on-board the fishing vessel, managed to cling on to a propeller and haul himself to shore. His son David, aged just 9, was swept out to sea. The battered wreck of the George Elmy was discovered upturned on an adjacent beach the following morning.

In 2009, 47 years after the disaster, the George Elmy was bought back to Seaham by the East Durham Heritage Group after being spotted for sale on Ebay. After four years of painstaking and dedicated restoration, the George Elmy was relaunched. Brian Salt of the group stated, "We have waited a long time, but we are delighted to have her home now".

The restored lifeboat returns to Seaham in 2013 (credit: East Durham Heritage & Lifeboat Centre)

Ipswich Town Win the League

Alf Ramsey will probably always be remembered for his achievements with England during the 1966 World Cup, but what he did as manager of Ipswich Town was equally remarkable. The Tractor Boys were in Division Three South when England's future World Cup-winning manager took charge in 1955. So began an incredible climb to the top. They gained promotion to the second tier in 1957 before winning the Division Two title in 1961. As if that wasn't enough, they won the League Championship in their first season in the top division, just as Ramsey had done as a player with Tottenham Hotspur eleven years earlier.

Alf Ramsey

Tottenham Hotspur retained the F.A. Cup by beating Burnley 3-1 in the final thus qualifying them for the European Cup Winners' Cup, which they would win the following season. In Scotland, Dundee won the league by 3 points from Rangers. Rangers did, however, gain some compensation by lifting both the Scottish Cup and the League Cup, beating St. Mirren and Hearts respectively.

The 1962 FIFA World Cup

When, in 1956, Chile held off the challenge of Argentina to host the World Cup, there was a great mood of optimism in the country. But no-one could have foreseen the Valdivia Earthquake, the most powerful ever recorded. As well as considerable loss of life and destruction to property, it left the Chilean government with greater priorities than the repair of sporting venues. It would have seemed wise to move the tournament to neighbouring Argentina, but fierce rivalry prevented this. The tournament went ahead with only the National Stadium in Santiago really fit to host matches.

The victorious Brazilian national football team

It still had a capacity of over 68,000 whilst regional venues could only cater for a fraction of the crowd. Astonishingly, a group match between Brazil and Mexico was played in front of a crowd of 10,484 in Estadio Sausalito. More people had gone to see Queens Park Rangers on a wet Wednesday evening that season. England squeaked through their group on goal average, heading for the knockout stages in an upbeat mood. It was there that they ran into defending champions Brazil. The footballer of the tournament and one of the all-time greats, Garrincha, scored twice in a 3-1 victory for the South Americans. Brazil then put four past Chile in the semis before meeting Czechoslovakia in the final. The Brazilians were nervous as the Czechs had held them to a draw in the group stages, plus the referee was from the Czechs' communist ally the Soviet Union. They needn't have worried as they ran out comfortable 3-1 winners to retain the trophy they had won four years earlier in Sweden.

Tennis

The 76th edition of the All England Lawn Tennis Championships was buzzing with talk of seasonal Grand Slams in both the ladies' and gentlemen's singles competitions. The two greatest Australians ever to play the game had both won the first two majors of the year. Margaret Smith, later better known by her married name Court, had already won the Australian and French Opens. She defeated fellow countrywomen Jan O'Neill on grass in Melbourne and Lesley Bowrey on clay in Paris. Rod Laver had also stood two and zero in the big events, twice defeating Roy Emerson. Everything seemed set fair for Smith to add to her tally. She received a bye into the second round, where she met the unseeded Billie Jean Moffit (later King), She looked to be cruising, taking the first set 6-1. Moffit fought back to win the next two sets, making Smith the first top seed to be eliminated in the

Australian champion Margaret Smith

first round of the ladies' singles. Moffit would only reach the quarter finals where she lost to Anne Haydon (later Jones). The eventual winner was Karen Susman, the girls' champion from 1960, who beat Czech Vera Sokova in the final. Laver faired better. After sailing through the top half of the draw without dropping a set, the men's top seed faced Manuel Santana in the quarter finals. After a gruelling 16-14 loss of the first set, Laver regained his composure to win the next three. He would not then drop another set and comfortably beat fellow countryman Martin Mulligan 6-2, 6-2 6-1 in the final. Laver would go on to complete a season's Grand Slam at the US National Championships at Forest Hill in New York. Soon after, he would turn his back on the amateur game by turning professional. He was banned from Grand Slam tennis for five years. In 1969, as if to prove a point, he completed another season Grand Slam. Without those missing five years Laver would undoubtedly have added many more majors which would have put him close to or beyond the records of Nadal,

1962 Wimbledon champion Rod Laver

Djokovic and Federer. Both Court (nee Smith) and Laver are part of a select few major winners to have tennis courts named after them. Arthur Ashe and Susan Lenglen have eponymous courts in the US and France respectively. Court and Laver were honoured in Australia. Sadly Henman Hill and Murray Mound do not count!

In the Davis Cup, (the international tournament for men) Britain trounced Brazil 4-1 in the Euro/Americas Zone quarter finals on grass at Eastbourne. However, they were no match for the Italians in the semis on clay in Milan, surrendering 5-0. The final was held between Australia and Mexico. Australia were the powerhouse of men's tennis, boasting three players who had been ranked number one. Rod Laver, Neale Fraser and Roy Emerson. Held on grass in Melbourne, the home side swept all before them in a 5-0 whitewash.

Rugby Union

If you were a fan of rugby union in the late 1950s or the early 1960s, you were really a fan. Tries were rarer than hens' teeth. 1962 saw England draw 0-0 with Wales in January, a feat that was matched in 1963 when they also shared a pointless draw with Ireland in Dublin. It is something that is unimaginable in the modern game. In fact some of the scorelines are somnambulating. Wales 0-3 England (1957), Scotland 3-3 England (1958), France 3-3 England (1960), Scotland 3-0 Wales (1961), Scotland 3-3 England, Wales 3-0 France, Ireland 3-3 Wales (1962).

Line-outs were frequent in games

When Scotland lost 6-0 to Wales at Murrayfield in 1963, there were an incredible 111 line-outs. Rugby Union was in an awful state, with defences on top and space for the more creative players at a premium. In 1959, England racked up a grand total of nine points in their four matches without crossing the line for a single try. Amazingly, they still avoided the wooden spoon. In doing so they became the first side to go through an entire Five Nations campaign without registering a single try.

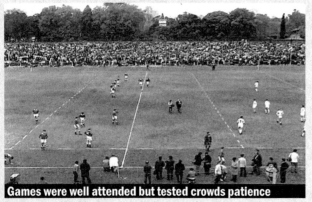

Games were well attended but tested crowds patience

Not to be outdone, in 1962 Wales matched England's woeful feat with nine points and no tries, again avoiding the wooden spoon. Reporter Denys Rowbotham, in a blistering rage, spoke of "the game's all but insufferable monotony ... nimble backs, who might have produced fireworks, were reduced to damp squibs by immediate suffocation. One of these days, defensive, characterless rugby will empty grounds".

Radical change was needed and rule changes were made. Players not involved in line-outs were moved 10 yards behind play, and offside at the scrum was defined by the furthest foot back, rather than the point of input. Although the scoreboards took a while to warm up properly, the days of the 0-0 draw were over.

The backs were "suffocated"

New rules brought change

Cricket

In November 1962 one of cricket's lingering anachronisms was finally scrapped. Until the growth of Test cricket and outside of an Ashes summer, the highlights of the season were the Gentlemen v Players matches. The splitting of players into two distinct groups was a fundamental part of the game. In its simplest form, professionals (known as players) were paid, amateurs (widely known as gentlemen) were not; however, many of the so-called amateurs earned more than their professional counterparts. The reality was that almost all gentlemen were public school educated or at least middle-class and the professionals were generally working-class. Professionals were often treated much as servants would be and were expected to be as deferential to Gentlemen and committeemen, as a butler would be to the master of the house. They had separate hotels when they travelled, separate changing rooms and food at the grounds, referred to by their surnames only, and at most counties could never aspire to captaincy. Even scorecards made a small but marked distinction; amateurs were given full initials, professionals surname only. Perhaps the way captaincy was handled was the most ridiculous aspect of it all. Professionals were deemed unable to take on such a role, and so often found themselves playing under amateur captains who were barely of club standard. Counties would scratch around to find someone, anyone, willing to take charge. Some were so poor that they did little more than stand on the field leaving the senior professionals to run the show. The match that finally brought the farce to an end took place in Scarborough. It was a three day match, starting on September 8th where the Players won convincingly by 7 wickets. Tony Lock and Fred Trueman (who was as working class as they come) shared 13 wickets between them with Ken Barrington scoring the only century of the game, all for the victors. Tony Lock's name will forever be etched in cricket history as he took the "other wicket" in 1956 at Old Trafford against Australia when Jim Laker took 19 for 90.

1962 Season Highlights

- The County Championship was won by Yorkshire.
- England beat Pakistan 4-0 in a five match series.
- Bill Alley did "the double" with 1915 runs and 112 wickets
- Fred Titmus and Mushtaq Mohammed were named amongst Wisden's five best cricketers of the year.

Professionals were often working class

Captains were always 'Gentlemen'

Gentlemen hailed from public school

Bill Alley

The Derby

Larkspur, ridden by Neville Sellwood, on his way to winning the 1962 Derby

The bare facts about the 1962 Epsom Derby, held on the first Wednesday in June, tell only half the story. Over half a million people attended the race which saw outsider Larkspur, ridden by Neville Sellwood and trained in Ireland by Vincent O'Brien, win the race by two lengths. The race was one of the most dramatic in the Derby's near 200 year history. 26 horses lined up and, in those days, they did not have the aid of starting stalls. As well as the size of the field, a big problem was that only five of the horses had proven form over anything further than a mile. There were simply too many speed horses in the race who were used to running on flatter, easier tracks than Epsom. When the starter let them go, the majority of the field set off at a blistering pace with the proven stayers finding themselves behind a wall of horses at the back of the field. This was a recipe for disaster; at the turn towards Tattenham Corner the field began to concertina. Seven horses fell or were brought down including the favourite Hethersett, 2000 Guineas runner up Romulus and the Lingfield Derby Trial winner Pindaric. Sadly one of the fallers, King Canute, broke a leg and had to be put down. In addition, six jockeys were taken to hospital. The Derby was made safer by the introduction of starting stalls in 1967 and the field was limited to 20 runners. It may not have been the way Vincent O'Brien wanted to win his first Derby, but the legendary Irish trainer has the rare distinction of training both Grand National and Derby winners. He won the National three times in the 1950s with three different horses and would go on to win a further five Derbies.

The Grand National

The Grand National took place on March 21st. The BBC, in its third year of broadcasting the event, produced a special Grandstand programme with David Coleman at the helm. Peter O'Sullivan led the commentary team, assisted by Peter Montague-Evans and Bob Haynes. The race was won by 28/1 shot Kilmore, ridden by Fred Winter. The favourite, Frenchman's Cove, ridden by champion jockey Stan Mellor, had no luck in running and was brought down at the 19th fence.

1962 Commonwealth Paraplegic Games

The post war years saw a burgeoning of disability sports, perhaps fuelled by the fact that so many men and women had been injured during the conflict. The Stoke Mandeville games first took place in 1948 in England, followed by the inaugural Paralympics in Rome in 1960. 1962 saw the first Paraplegic Games, which were held prior to the British Empire and Commonwealth

1962 Commonwealth Paraplegic Games Competitors

Games in Perth, Australia. The city was very supportive of the games, both in terms of attending events and extensive news coverage. The emblem of the games, a wheelchair athlete throwing a javelin with the Australian flag in the background, was found on the Games flag, competition medals, the programme and the tickets. Events included archery, basketball, club throw, fencing, javelin throw, pentathlon, precision javelin, shot put, snooker, swimming, table tennis and weightlifting. Out of the 13 events available to athletes, weightlifting was of special significance due to the fact that national and international records were established in Perth. The Australian team consisted of 24 athletes, 3 women and 21 men. They won 38 gold medals in total. Noteworthy performances were given by Daphne Ceeney, a founding member of the Paraplegic Sports Club of New South Wales, who won eight gold medals across seven disciplines. Lorraine Dodd set two world records in backstroke and freestyle swimming, winning seven gold medals. Frank Ponta won more medals than any other competitor, with a total haul of eleven medals.

Cycling - Beryl Burton

Beryl Burton is the greatest sportsperson you have probably never heard of. In 1962 she won the world championship, as she did in so many other years. No other British sportswoman has dominated their field in the way that Beryl Burton dominated the world of cycling. As Velo Gotha, the Belgian-published bible of cycling facts and figures succinctly puts it: "She was the best known and most successful woman cyclist." In the course of a career that spanned five decades, the fiercely competitive Yorkshirewoman won seven world titles, two road race championships, five track pursuit titles, 96 national titles, 12 road race championships, 13 pursuit titles and 71 time trial titles against the clock. She also won all-rounder titles, awarded to the fastest woman against the watch over 25, 50 and 100 mile distances. Along the way she set speed records, supervised her own training,

Beryl Burton

rode the races she wanted and had little to do with the sport's governing bodies. But her achievements were impossible to ignore and she was awarded an MBE in 1964, and an OBE in 1968. Despite such recognition Burton never felt that either the local or national press properly appreciated her efforts. She may have had a point since, when she was at the peak of her powers, she regularly beat the men. In 1967, she overtook Mike McNamara in an Otley CC 12-hour time trial on her way to setting a women's record of 277.25 miles in the set time. McNamara's distance of 276.52 miles in the same event was itself a new men's record.

Floyd Patterson versus Sonny Liston

Comiskey Park, Chicago
September 25th 1962

The 1960s was a time of great boxing writing: think Harry Carpenter, Reg Gutteridge and Harry Gibbs. It was also a time when great writers were magnetically attracted to boxing. Two of America's greatest writers, Norman Mailer and James Baldwin, attended the fight of the year. The contest for the World Heavyweight crown pitted champion Floyd Patterson against challenger Charles "Sonny" Liston. In a poll, 64 of 102 reporters picked Patterson to win as did several former champions like Rocky Marciano and Ingemar Johannson. A young boxer by the name of Cassius Clay, later Muhammed Ali, picked Liston to win inside five rounds. Clay was right, the fight was a mismatch. The challenger used his 25lb weight advantage to knock out the champion after 2 minutes and 6 seconds of the first round. Norman Mailer, in his essay *Ten Thousand Words a Minute*, contrasted the silent giant Liston with the more jovial Patterson. He cast the fight as one with a clear villain and hero, using derogatory language. He also saw it as somehow mirroring the civil rights struggles in America, and as was usual with Mailer, he placed himself at the centre of the story. Baldwin was more eloquent and succinct when he wrote that Liston was "inarticulate in the way we all are when more has happened to us than we know how to express."

Sonny Liston

Liston knocks out Patterson

Liston would fight Patterson again the following July in Las Vegas. That fight lasted only four seconds longer than the original with Patterson, now the challenger, hitting the canvas three times in the first round. Liston now seemed unbeatable. That was until the young pretender, a certain Cassius Clay, stepped into the ring with him in 1964 and produced one of the biggest upsets in the sport's history.

Floyd Patterson

Golf

The Open | Royal Troon, Scotland 11th to 13th July 1962

No matter that Arnold Palmer was the world's greatest golfer and also defending champion, like all the other competitors in the 1962 Open, he had to qualify. Qualifying took place over 36 holes at the Old Course at Royal Troon and at Lochgreen Municipal Course. Scotland's Eric Brown led the qualifiers with 139, Palmer played it safe coming in four shots behind. The champ had attracted large crowds when he won at Royal Birkdale, but even bigger crowds swarmed over Troon. Palmer had also encouraged many of his fellow Americans to make the journey over the Atlantic. These included Phil Rodgers, Gene Littler and the 22-year-old US Open Champion, a certain Jack Nicklaus. In The Open proper, Nicklaus, who was to become the most successful Major winning golfer of all time had a bit of a nightmare. A 10 at the 11th hole and rounds of 79 and 80 contributed to him finishing 34th. He would rarely be out of the top 3 in the following two decades. After the first round, England's Keith MacDonald led the way with a 3-under par 69. Lurking two shots back were the 1960 champion, Australian Ken Nagle, and Palmer. Thereafter, Palmer played almost flawless golf. A second round 69 put him two clear of Nagle and a third round 67 saw him stretch the lead by a further 3 shots. He closed out with a 69 to win by a comfortable 6 shots. His combined four round score of 276 beat the old record by 2 shots. It was a record that would stand until Tom Watson won the Open at Turnberry in 1977. Gary Player, another future great of the game, missed the cut. Peter Alliss, the future voice of golf, tied 8th, a whopping 17 shots off the winner. Palmer had not only cemented his position as one of the game's all-time greats but, by encouraging so many Americans to come over, he also helped re-establish The Open as golf's leading major.

Royal Troon Golf Club

Arnold Palmer

Other Major Events

In The Masters at Augusta, Palmer let a 3-shot lead slip in the final round but won in a play-off with Gary player and Dow Finsterwald. Player won the USPGA and Jack Nicklaus beat Palmer in a play-off to win the US Open. The year's women's US Open was won by American Murle Lindstom. Even though her prize of $1800 was a fraction of the men's, golf was one of very few sports where women could make a living.

Gary Player with his wife

Motor Racing

The early 1960s were a golden age for Formula 1. The sport, which started in 1950, pitted the the most talented drivers in the fastest regulated racecourse cars against each other. F1 was raw, exciting and glamorous, but also extremely dangerous as man and machine were pushed to their limits. In 1961, American Phil Hill won his only world championship for Ferrari after his teammate and close rival, Wolfgang von Trips, was killed at the Italian Grand Prix in the penultimate race of the season. The 1961 season was a poor one for the leading British team, British Racing Motors (BRM). They had been caught off guard by new

Graham Hill wins the Dutch Grand Prix at Zandvoort

Jim Clark in the groundbreaking Lotus 25

regulations limiting engine size to 1.5 litres. By the beginning of the 1962 season the design team of Richard Mays and Peter Burton had produced the BRM P57, a car to rival any of the other British and Continental opposition. The season ran from May 20th when BRM driver Graham Hill won the Dutch Grand Prix at Zandvoort, to 29th December when Hill was crowned world champion at Prince George, South Africa. That he only managed one pole position out of the nine races is testament, not only to the great manoeuvrability of the car, but also to the skill of Hill as a driver. He left in his wake two of the greatest names in British motor sport history, Jim Clark and John Surtees. Clark may have felt hard done by as he managed six pole positions throughout the season and dominated the final race from the start. On the 20th lap, when leading, his Lotus car failed him forcing him to retire due to engine failure. This left the path clear for Hill to take the chequered flag and to also lift the world championship. The glitz of motor racing was not lost on the film industry and they tried to cash in on its popularity with mixed success. James Bond always drove the fastest most expensive cars of the age. However, the silver screen's love affair with all things fast was not always successful. Made in 1962 and released the following year, the American film *The Checkered Flag*, a murder mystery, has made it into the hall of fame as one of the worst movies ever produced. In it, the alcoholic wife of a successful racing driver persuades another driver to kill her husband. As if motor racing was not dangerous enough!

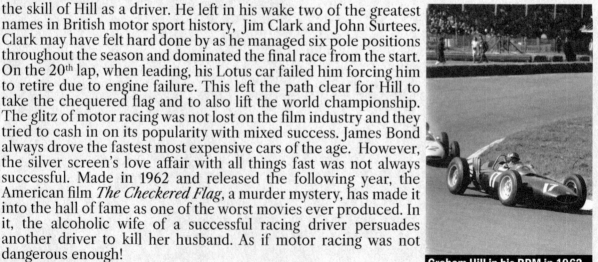

Graham Hill in his BRM in 1962

BBC Sports Personality of the Year

The BBC Sports Personality of the Year Award was the brainchild of Paul Fox who was the editor of the popular BBC show, Sportsview. Voted for by the general public by postcard, the first award was presented in 1954 to Christopher Chataway who beat fellow athlete Roger Bannister. Throughout its history the award has not been without controversy. There have been several attempts to get the sport of angling recognised, but the award's administrators judged the votes sent in to be invalid. Athletes are far and away the most frequent winners of the trophy, followed by racing drivers and then tennis players. In 1962 swimmer Anita Lonsbrough was the first female winner of what was then known as the Sportsview Personality of the Year Award. Aged 21, she won Commonwealth Games gold medals in the 110 yards breaststroke, the 220 yards breaststroke and the 440 yards individual medley. This added to the 200m breaststroke gold medal she secured at the 1960 Rome Olympics. Lonsbrough went on to become Great Britain's first female Olympic flag bearer at the opening ceremony of the Summer Games in Tokyo in 1964. Throughout her career she broke five world records and won seven gold medals. Upon retirement she became a respected sports journalist for the Daily Telegraph.

Anita Lonsbrough won the award

Sprinter Dorothy Hyman came second. She had her most successful season in 1962, winning gold in the 100m at the European Championships in Belgrade as well as completing the sprint double of 110yds and 220yds at the Commonwealth Games in Perth, Western Australia. Hyman was to gain compensation the following year when she won the award. In 1964 she decided to retire from the sport aged just 23. Her retirement was hastened by the intended publication of her autobiography, entitled Sprint, as earnings from the book would have invalidated her amateur status. It was a clean sweep for female athletes as another swimmer, Linda Ludgrove, took third place. She won two individual backstroke medals in the 110yds and 220yds at the Commonwealth Games. Throughout her career she broke seven world records. The World Sports Star of the Year went to Canadian figure skater Donald Jackson who won the World Championship in Prague. During the competition he became the first skater in history to successfully land a triple Lutz jump in competition. The Team of the Year Award went to the BRM racing team who won the F1 constructors' title as well as their driver, Graham Hill, winning the individual title.

Sprinter Dorothy Hyman came 2nd

Swimmer Linda Ludgrove came 3rd

The Lotus Type 26 Drop Head Coupé better known as the Lotus Elan went on sale in 1962. It was designed by Ron Hickman, who also designed the Black and Decker Workmate. This model is the Lotus Elan 1600 S1 with rare hardtop.

The BMC AD016 was a range of cars launched in 1962 by the British Motor Corporation, marketed under various brands including Austin, Morris, MG, Riley and Vanden Plas. This car is the Austin 1100 Mk.1. The Austin 1100 Countryman was the car Basil Fawlty gave 'a damn good thrashing'. The AD016 was Britain's best selling car from 1963-66 and 1968-71.

This is the Lockheed A-12 high-altitude reconnaissance jet built for the United States Central Intelligence Agency by Lockheed. Capable of Mach 3+ (over 2300mph), it first flew in 1962. It was the precursor to the SR-71 Blackbird.

The Aero Spacelines Pregnant Guppy was a wide-bodied cargo aircraft built in the USA and used for ferrying outsized cargo items including rocket components for NASA. When it first flew in 1962 it was the largest plane in the world.

The Agfa Optima 1a was one of the first fully automatic scale-focusing 35mm film cameras. Launched in 1962, it incorporated a selenium cell to measure light levels and power the automatic aperture setting and shutter speed.

The Braun FS5 television, launched in 1962, is the work of designer Dieter Rams and his team. His design philosophy of "Less, but better" inspired generations of designers, most notably Jonathan Ive, former chief designer officer at Apple.

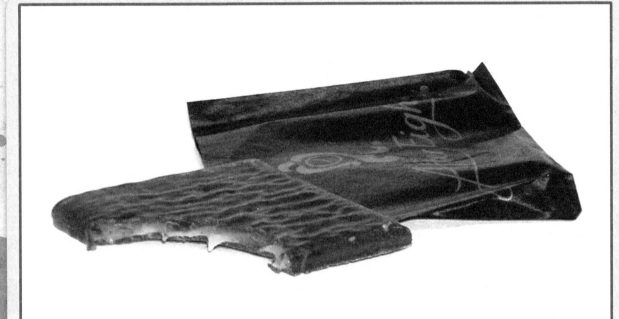

After Eight Mint Chocolate Thins were created by the Rowntree Company in 1962. The mint chocolate covered sugar confectionery was originally produced in York. Nowadays over 1 billion After Eight mints are produced every year.

The Topic chocolate bar was introduced in the UK by Mars Incorporated in 1962 and advertised with the tagline "A Hazelnut in Every Bite". The bar contains hazelnuts, nougat and caramel with a milk chocolate coating.

Photo Credits

Credits shown in the order in which they appear in the book. Photos not listed are in the public domain.

Key to page numbers

fc = front cover; **tp** = title page; **cp** = contents page; **ap1** = acknowledgements page 1; **ap2** = acknowledgements page 2; **rop** = reader offer page; **ibc** = inside back cover; **bc** = back cover; **3** = page 3; **4** = page 4; etc.

Key to object position on page

tl = top left; *t* = top; *tc* = top centre; *tr* = top right; *cla* = centre left above; *ca* = centre above; *cra* = centre right above; *cl* = centre left; *c* = centre; *cr* = centre right; *clb* = centre left below; *cb* = centre below; *crb* = centre right below; *bl* = bottom left; *b* = bottom; *bc* = bottom centre; *br* = bottom right; *w* = whole page; *h* = header; *tb* = text background

Key to image licence types

CC BY-SA 2.0 = https://creativecommons.org/licenses/by-sa/2.0/deed.en;
CC BY-SA 3.0 = https://creativecommons.org/licenses/by-sa/3.0/deed.en;
CC BY-SA 4.0 = https://creativecommons.org/licenses/by-sa/4.0/deed.en;
(m) = image has been modified as permitted under licensing terms

fc *cla*: Graham Hill (m) © Joop Van Bilsen/ Anefo, Wikimedia Commons, CC BY-SA 3.0; **fc** *crb*: Jim Clark (m) © Joop Van Bilsen/ Anefo, Wikimedia Commons, CC BY-SA 3.0; **fc** *br*: Pele (m) © Joop Van Bilsen/ Anefo, Wikimedia Commons, CC BY-SA 3.0; **tp** *w*: Jaguar E-Type (m) © Martin Brazill / Shutterstock.com; **2** *tc*: Ladies dancing, kind permission of Jenny Finch; **3** *tc*: Radio Butlin, kind permission of Jenny Finch; **4** *cla*: Frozen Road, © Howard Dublin, Wikimedia Commons, CC BY-SA 4.0; **16** *cla*: Hugh Dennis © The National Churches Trust, Wikimedia Commons, CC BY-SA 2.0; **17** *cla*: Steve Redgrave © Brunel University, Flickr, CC BY-SA 2.0; **17** *clb*: Richard Coles © Phil Guest, Wikimedia Commons, CC BY-SA 2.0; **18** *cla*: Phillip Schofield © The home of Fixers, Flickr, CC BY-SA 2.0; **18** *clb*: Evan Davis © Policy Exchange, Wikimedia Commons, CC BY-SA 2.0; **19** *cla*: Michelle Collins © Featureflash Photo Agency / Shutterstock.com; **19** *clb*: Eamonn Walker © s_bukley / Shutterstock.com; **20** *cla*: Tom Cruise © Dick Thomas Johnson, Wikimedia Commons, CC BY-SA 2.0; **20** *clb*: Neil Morrissey © Emilie Fjola Sandy/BBC Archive; **21** *cla*: Tracy Edwards © The Maiden Factor; **21** *clb*: Jim Al-Khalili © Duncan.Hull, Wikimedia Commons, CC BY-SA 3.0; **22** *cla*: Tracey Thorn © Edwardmbishop, Wikimedia Commons, CC BY-SA 4.0; **22** *clb*: Jodie Foster © DFree / Shutterstock.com; **23** *cla*: Ralph Fiennes © Dick Thomas Johnson, Wikimedia Commons, CC BY-SA 2.0; **23** *clb row 1*: Jim Carrey © Ian Smith, Wikimedia Commons, CC BY-SA 2.0; **23** *cb row 1*: Axl Rose © Ed Vill, Wikimedia Commons, CC BY-SA 2.0; **23** *crb row 1*: Eddie Izzard © Christopher William Adach, Wikimedia Commons, CC BY-SA 2.0; **23** *clb row 2*: Vanessa Feltz © Raph_PH, Wikimedia Commons, CC BY-SA 2.0; **23** *cb row 2*: John Hannah © Gage Skidmore, Wikimedia Commons, CC BY-SA 3.0; **23** *crb row 2*: Stuart Pearce © Doha Stadium Plus Qatar, Wikimedia Commons, CC BY-SA 2.0; **23** *clb row 3*: Jimmy White © Benutzer:Bill da Flute, Wikimedia Commons, CC BY-SA 3.0; **23** *cb row 3*: Paula Abdul © Alison Martin, Wikimedia Commons, CC BY-SA 2.0; **23** *crb row 3*: Phill Jupitus © Auntiep69, Wikimedia Commons, CC BY-SA 4.0; **23** *clb row 4*: Michael Ball © aunt agatha, Wikimedia Commons, CC BY-SA 2.0; **23** *cb row 4*: Amanda Donohoe © Featureflash Photo Agency / Shutterstock.com; **23** *crb row 4*: Shaun Ryder © Featureflash Photo Agency / Shutterstock.com; **23** *clb row 5*: Steve Irwin © Australia Zoo Pty Ltd, Wikimedia Commons, CC BY-SA 1.0; **23** *cb row 5*: John Fashanu © Featureflash Photo Agency / Shutterstock.com; **23** *crb row 5*: Demi Moore © David Shankbone, Wikimedia Commons, CC BY-SA 2.0; **24** *cl*: Vita Sackville-West © DHRUVA SRINIVAS, Wikimedia Commons, CC BY-SA 4.0; **27** *tl*: Coins © Jo Smiley Hailey, Unsplash.com; **27** *tr*: House © Sludgegulper, Wikimedia Commons, CC BY-SA 2.0; **27** *cl*: Ford Cortina © Charles01, Wikimedia Commons, CC BY-SA 3.0; **27** *bl*: Typewriter © Rainer P. A. Wermke, Wikimedia Commons, CC BY-SA 4.0; **27** *bc*: Bread © Dmitry Makeev, Wikimedia Commons, CC BY-SA 2.0; **27** *br*: Petrol Station © Erik Mclean, Unsplash.com; **28** *tr*: Malaysian plantation kindly supplied by ex-Plantation Manager John Lewis; **30** *tc*: IR8 Seeds © IRRI (www.irri.org), Wikimedia Commons, CC BY-SA 3.0; **30** *tr*: Barrels © Bbadgett, Wikimedia Commons, CC BY-SA 3.0; **33** *br*: Barbie © Nelson Tiffany, Los Angeles Times, Wikimedia Commons, CC BY-SA 4.0; **36** *cra*: Gratin Dauphinois © Ludovic Péron, Wikimedia Commons, CC BY-SA 3.0; **37** *c*: Spotted Dick © Tracy, Wikimedia Commons, CC BY-SA 2.0; **38** *cra*: SS Canberra © John Ward, Wikimedia Commons, CC BY-SA 4.0; **39** *all images*: © with thanks to Jenny Finch; **45** *clb*: Cruise ship © Image: Freepik.com; **45** *clb*: Mermaid © Image: Freepik.com; **45** *clb*: Life Ring © Image: OpenClipart-Vectors from Pixabay; **46** *clb*: Z Cars © BBC Archive; **47** *tl*: Bamber Gascoigne © Christina Gascoigne, Wikimedia Commons, CC BY-SA 3.0; **48** *tl*: Animal Magic © BBC Archive; **48** *clb*: Steptoe and Son © BBC Archive; **49** *tr*: BBC Broadcasting House © Redvers, Wikimedia Commons, CC BY-SA 3.0; **50** *cl*: Frank Ifield © Bradford Timeline, Flickr, CC BY-SA 2.0; **51** *bl*: Bernard Cribbins © Bradford Timeline, Flickr, CC BY-SA 2.0; **54** *br*: The Marquee Club © Kiwi, Wikimedia Commons, CC BY-SA 3.0; **55** *tr*: Norman Vaughan © Bradford Timeline, Flickr, CC BY-SA 2.0; **55** *br*: Eartha Kitt © Boris Carmi /Meitar Collection / National Library of Israel / The Pritzker Family National Photography Collection, Wikimedia Commons, CC BY-SA 4.0; **55** *bl*: Frank Ifield © Bradford Timeline, Flickr, CC BY-SA 2.0; **55** *bc*: Bob Hope © Carl Albert Research and Studies Center, Congressional Collection, Wikimedia Commons, CC BY-SA 4.0; **56** *cl*: Stevie Smith © Akshay Nagaraju B, Wikimedia Commons, CC BY-SA 4.0; **56** *br*: Andy Warhol © Jack Mitchell, Wikimedia Commons, CC BY-SA 4.0; **57** *cl*: Pills © Towfiqu barbhuiya, Unsplash.com; **57** *bl*: Prison © Tim Hüfner, Unsplash; **58** *tl*: Building (m) © Rachel Martin, Unsplash; **58** *cl*: Notebook © Bookblock, Unsplash; **58** *bl*: Horse © Daniel Bonilla, Unsplash; **59** *tl*: Child sleeping © Annie Spratt, Unsplash; **59** *bl*: Enchanted Wood © Oliver Roos, Unsplash; **60** *tl*: Paul Scofield © Allan warren, Wikimedia Commons, CC BY-SA 3.0; **61** *br*: Carol Ann Duffy © walnut whippet, Wikimedia Commons, CC BY-SA 2.0; **62** *tl*: Atlas computer © Iain MacCallum, Wikimedia Commons, CC BY-SA 3.0; **63** *tc*: PDP-1 Control Panel © Takuya Oikawa, Wikimedia Commons, CC BY-SA 2.0; **63** *tr*: Spacewar game © Kenneth Lu, Wikimedia Commons, CC BY-SA 2.0; **63** *clb*: Cassette © Thegreenj, Wikimedia Commons, CC BY-SA 3.0; **64** *tl*: Telstar-1 © Rama, Wikimedia Commons, CC BY-SA 3.0; **64** *tl*: Space © NASA, Unsplash; **65** *bl*: Quasar © ESA/Hubble & NASA, Wikimedia Commons, CC BY-SA 4.0; **66** *bl*: Propanolol tablets © Garzfoth, Wikimedia Commons, CC BY-SA 4.0; **67** *tr*: Space Needle © Seattle Municipal Archives, Wikimedia Commons, CC BY-SA 2.0; **67** *GM* stand © Seattle Municipal Archives, Wikimedia Commons, CC BY-SA 2.0; **67** *br*: Monorail © Seattle Municipal Archives, Wikimedia Commons, CC BY-SA 2.0; **69** *tr*: East Dundry Lane © HowardDublin, Wikimedia Commons, CC BY-SA 4.0; **69** *cl*: Old Farm © Richard Johnson, Wikimedia Commons, CC BY-SA 2.0; **69** *br*: Ormerod House© Richard Johnson, Wikimedia Commons, CC BY-SA 2.0; **70** *cla*: Hamburg Flood © Gerhard Pietsch, Wikimedia Commons, CC BY-SA 3.0;

Photo Credits continued

72 *tr*: Coppenhall Junction Crash © PA Images / Alamy Stock Photo; 73 *br*: Eichman walking in prison © National Photo Collection of Israel, Wikimedia Commons, CC BY-SA 3.0; 74 *cl*: Avalanche © Simon, Pixabay; 74 *crb*: Yungay Cathedral © Zafiroblue05, Wikimedia Commons, CC BY-SA 3.0; 75 *tr*: Wild Sea © Michael Krahn, Unsplash; 75 *cl*: George Elmy washed up © www.eastdurhamheritagegroup.co.uk; 75 *br*: George Elmy returns © www.eastdurhamheritagegroup.co.uk; 76 *tr*: Alf Ramsey © Bert Verhoeff / Anefo, Wikimedia Commons, CC BY-SA 3.0; 80 *t*: 1962 Derby © PA Images / Alamy Stock Photo; 81 *tr*: Paraplegic Games Competitors (m) © Daphne Ceeney/Australian Paralympic Committee, Wikimedia Commons, CC BY-SA 1.0; 81 *crb*: Beryl Burton (m) © Kroon, Ron / Anefo, Wikimedia Commons, CC BY-SA 3.0; 82 *cl*: Sonny Liston (m) © Mick Baker/rooster, Flickr, CC BY-ND 2.0; 83 *tr*: Royal Troon (m) © Chris Morgan, Wikimedia Commons, CC BY-SA 2.0; 84 *tr*: Graham Hill (m) © Bilsen, Joop van / Anefo, Wikimedia Commons, CC BY-SA 3.0; 84 *cl*: Jim Clark (m) © Bilsen, Joop van / Anefo, Wikimedia Commons, CC BY-SA 3.0; 85 *tr*: Anita Lonsbrough (m) © PA Images / Alamy Stock Photo; 86 *t*: Lotus Elan (m) © dave_7, Wikimedia Commons, CC BY-SA 2.0; 86 *b*: Austin 1100 (m) © Charles01, Wikimedia Commons, CC BY-SA 3.0; 88 *t*: Agfa Optima (m) © CEphoto, Uwe Aranas, Wikimedia Commons, CC BY-SA 2.0; 92 *tc*: Coffee Table (m) © Sincerely Media, Unsplash.com; **BC** *tr*: Queen Elizabeth at the Chelsea Flower Show (m) © Karen Roe, Flickr, CC BY-SA 2.0;

Graphic and Background Image Credits

Credits shown in the order in which they appear in the book.

Additional Key

(ic) = icon; (ph) = photo

fc *c*, **tp** *ca*, **bc** *w*: (ph) Texture by Felipe Santana, Unsplash; *cp*, 3-15: (ph) Wood by Michael Schwarzenberger, Pixabay; 2-3, 16-92 *tb*: (m)(ph) Paper Texture by rawpixel.com; 3 *cla*: (ic) Play by Adrien Coquet, thenounproject.com, CC BY-SA 2.0; 6,8,10,12,14 *tl* & 7,9,11,13,15 *tr*: (ic) Newspaper by Loic Poivet, thenounproject.com, CC BY-SA 2.0; 6-15 *c*: (ph) Book by Robert Armstrong, Pixabay; 16-25,42-61,86-92 *w*: (m)(ph) Concrete texture by rawpixel.com; 16,18,20,22 *tl* & 17,19,21,23 *tr*: (ic) Birthday Calendar by Kiran Shastry, thenounproject.com, CC BY-SA 2.0; 16 *cla*: (ic) Theatre Comedy by B Farias, thenounproject.com, CC BY-SA 2.0; 16,17 *clb* & 22 *cla*: (ic) Music Note by Karen Tyler, thenounproject.com, CC BY-SA 2.0; 17 *cla*: (ic) Rowing by Creative Stall, thenounproject.com, CC BY-SA 2.0; 18 *cla* & 18 *clb*: (ic) TV Presenter by Adrien Coquet, thenounproject.com, CC BY-SA 2.0; 19 *cla* & 19,20 *clb*: (ic) Theatre by Ben Davis, thenounproject.com, CC BY-SA 2.0; 20,23 *cla* & 22 *clb* & 24,25 *bl*: (ic) Clapper Board by Andrew Nielsen, thenounproject.com, CC BY-SA 2.0; 21 *cla*: (ic) Yacht by zaenul yahya, thenounproject.com, CC BY-SA 2.0; 21 *clb* & 25 *cl*: (ic) Physics by Jan Niklas Prause, thenounproject.com, CC BY-SA 2.0; 23 *clb*: (ic) Baby by Emily Keller, thenounproject.com, CC BY-SA 2.0; 24 *tl*: (ic) Wreath by Alex Muravev, thenounproject.com, CC BY-SA 2.0; 24 *tl*: (ic) Gangster by Adrien Coquet, thenounproject.com, CC BY-SA 2.0; 24 *cl* & 25 *tl*: (ic) Book by Travis Avery, thenounproject.com, CC BY-SA 2.0; 26 *tl* & 27 *tr*: (ic) Coins by Evgenii Likhachov, thenounproject.com, CC BY-SA 2.0; 26-40 *w*: (m)(ph) White Concrete Wall by rawpixel.com; 28 *tl*: (ic) Earth by David Khai, thenounproject.com, CC BY-SA 2.0; 29 *tr*: (ic) Office by Anggara Putra, thenounproject.com, CC BY-SA 2.0; 30 *tl*: (ic) Tractor by Olivier Guin, thenounproject.com, CC BY-SA 2.0; 31 *tr*: (ic) School Desk by Jongrak, thenounproject.com, CC BY-SA 2.0; 32 *tl*: (ic) Exams by Arjan Farzkenari, thenounproject.com, CC BY-SA 2.0; 33 *tr*: (ic) Children by IronSV, thenounproject.com, CC BY-SA 2.0; 34 *tl* & 35 *tr*: (ic) Home by Numero Uno, thenounproject.com, CC BY-SA 2.0; 36 *tl*: (ic) Potato by Firza Alamsyah, thenounproject.com, CC BY-SA 2.0; 37 *tr*: (ic) Pudding by Ranah Pixel Studio, thenounproject.com, CC BY-SA 2.0; 38 *tl* & 39 *tr*: (ic) Holiday by Claudia Revalinap, thenounproject.com, CC BY-SA 2.0; 40 *tl*: (ic) Fashion by Mahmure Alp, thenounproject.com, CC BY-SA 2.0; 41 *tr*: (ic) Christmas Tree by Azam Ishaq, thenounproject.com, CC BY-SA 2.0; 41 *w*: Christmas (m) © Annie Spratt, Unsplash.com; 42 *tl*: (ic) Entertainment by shashank singh, thenounproject.com, CC BY-SA 2.0; 43,45 *tr* & 44 *tl*: (ic) Clapper Board by Andrew Nielsen, thenounproject.com, CC BY-SA 2.0; 46 *tl* & 43,45 *tr*: (ic) Old TV by Eko Purnomo, thenounproject.com, CC BY-SA 2.0; 49 *tr*: (ic) Radio by GreenHill, thenounproject.com, CC BY-SA 2.0; 50,52 *tl* & 51 *tr*: (ic) Record by Mourad Mokrane, thenounproject.com, CC BY-SA 2.0; 53 *tr*: (ic) Music Note by Karen Tyler, thenounproject.com, CC BY-SA 2.0; 54 *tl* & 55 *tr*: (ic) Trumpet by Valter Bispo, thenounproject.com, CC BY-SA 2.0; 56 *tl*: (ic) Arts by Kelsey Armstrong, thenounproject.com, CC BY-SA 2.0; 57,59 *tr* & 58 *tl*: (ic) Book by Travis Avery, thenounproject.com, CC BY-SA 2.0; 60 *tl*: (ic) Theatre by Ben Davis, thenounproject.com, CC BY-SA 2.0; 61 *tr*: (ic) Poetry by Martin, thenounproject.com, CC BY-SA 2.0; 62-67 *w*: (ph) Electricity (m) © Hal Gatewood, Unsplash.com; 62 *tl*: (ic) Computer by Juicy Fish, thenounproject.com, CC BY-SA 2.0; 63 *tr*: (ic) Gamepad by Symbolon, thenounproject.com, CC BY-SA 2.0; 64 *tl* & 65 *tr*: (ic) Saturn by Trevor Dsouza, thenounproject.com, CC BY-SA 2.0; 66 *tl*: (ic) Medicine Bottle by Muhammad Nur Auliady Pamungkas, thenounproject.com, CC BY-SA 2.0; 67 *tr*: (ic) Fair by Amethyst Studio, thenounproject.com, CC BY-SA 2.0; 68 *tl*: (ic) Missiles by Hasan, thenounproject.com, CC BY-SA 2.0; 69 *tr*: (ic) Snowflake by Adrien Coquet, thenounproject.com, CC BY-SA 2.0; 69 *w*: (ph) Snowscape (m) © Craig Whitehead, Unsplash; 70 *tl*: (ic) Flooded House by wira wianda, thenounproject.com, CC BY-SA 2.0; 70 *w*: (ph) Sea Flooding (m) © Colby Winfield, Unsplash; 71 *tr*: (ic) Knives by Federico Panzano, thenounproject.com, CC BY-SA 2.0; 71 *w*: (ph) Houses of Parliament © vwalakte, Freepik; 72 *tl*: (ic) Train by Sierra Pennala, thenounproject.com, CC BY-SA 2.0; 72 *w*: (ph) Train Tracks (m) © Ben Garratt, Unsplash; 73 *tr*: (ic) Justice by LUTFI GANI AL ACHMAD, thenounproject.com, CC BY-SA 2.0; 73 *w*: (ph) Gallows (m) © Johannes Blenke, Freepik; 74 *tl*: (ic) Mountain by leo-graph.com, thenounproject.com, CC BY-SA 2.0; 74 *w*: (ph) Mountain Snow (m) © Jacky Barrit, Pixabay; 75 *tr*: (ic) Life Ring by Made, thenounproject.com, CC BY-SA 2.0; 75 *w*: (ph): Sea (m) © Matt Hardy, Unsplash; 76 *tl*: (ic) Football by leo-graph.com, thenounproject.com, CC BY-SA 2.0; 76 *w*: (ph) Football Pitch (m) © Alberto Frías, Unsplash.com; 77 *tr*: (ic) Tennis by Mister Pixel, thenounproject.com, CC BY-SA 2.0; 77 *w*: (ph) Tennis Court (m) © M. Z., Unsplash.com; 78 *tl*: (ic) Rugby Ball by Marco Livolsi, thenounproject.com, CC BY-SA 2.0; 78 *w*: (ph) Rugby Match (m) © Alex Motoc, Unsplash.com; 78 *h*: (ph) Rugby Lineout © Auckland Museum, Wikimedia Commons, CC BY-SA 4.0; 79 *tr*: (ic) Cricket by Bernd Lakenbrink, thenounproject.com, CC BY-SA 2.0; 79 *w*: (ph) Cricketer (m) © Yogendra Singh, Unsplash.com; 80 *tl*: (ic) Horse Racing by Sergio Morozov, thenounproject.com, CC BY-SA 2.0; 80 *w*: (ph) Racehorse (m) © Luisa Peter, Unsplash.com; 80 *h*: (ph) Horse Race © Jongsun Lee, Wikimedia Commons, CC BY-SA 3.0; 81 *tr*: (ic) Paralympics by ProSymbols, thenounproject.com, CC BY-SA 2.0; 81 *tr*: (ic) Cycling by Monika, thenounproject.com, CC BY-SA 2.0; 81 *h* & *b*: (ph) Wheelchair Basketball © Rachel Martin, Unsplash; 81 *h*: (ph) Cycling © Fritz Cohen, Flickr, CC BY-SA 3.0; 81 *b*: (ph) Cycle Race (m) © Quino Al, Unsplash.com; 82 *tl*: (ic) Boxing Glove by Anton Anuchin, thenounproject.com, CC BY-SA 2.0; 82 *w*: (ph) Boxing Match (m) © Johann Walter Bantz, Unsplash.com; 83 *tr*: (ic) Golfer by Nicolas Vicent, thenounproject.com, CC BY-SA 2.0; 83 *w*: (ph) Golfing (m) © Courtney Cook, Unsplash.com; 83 *h*: (ph) Golf Ball (m) © mk. s, Unsplash.com; 84 *tl*: (ic) Racing Car by Slidicon, thenounproject.com, CC BY-SA 2.0; 84 *w*: (ph) Chequered Flag (m) © Bas van den Eijkhof, Unsplash.com; 84 *h*: (ph) Race car (m) © Jeff Cooper, Unsplash.com; 85 *tr*: (ic) Trophy by Milinda Courey, thenounproject.com, CC BY-SA 2.0; 85 *w*: (ph) Trophies (m) © Courtney Cook, Unsplash.com; 86,88 *tl* & 87,89 *tr*: (ic) Framed Picture by Lil Squid, thenounproject.com, CC BY-SA 2.0; 90 *tl* & 91 *tr*: (ic) Camera by AomAm, thenounproject.com, CC BY-SA 2.0; 92 *tl*: (ic) Present by Vinzence Studio, thenounproject.com, CC BY-SA 2.0

Join us for news on our future releases, reader promotions and behind-the-scenes content. All at:

www.subscribepage.com/join1962

It's completely free to join. As a subscriber, we will email you no more than once or twice a month. We will never share your email address and you can unsubscribe at any time.

Answers to the Eleven-plus Exam on page 32

Arithmetic Questions

Q1: London to Birmingham is 120 miles
Q2: Christmas Day will fall on a Thursday
Q3: It will take 6 hours and 40 minutes
Q4: Five hundred and twenty three
Q5: A) John's mother was 40 years old
Q5: B) In 3 years' time
Q5: C) John will be 30 years old

General English Questions

Q1: A) Our dogs are carrying sticks.
Q1: B) Their butchers have no meat.
Q1: C) Men who like football are sure to have team scarves in their houses.
Q2: A) Finger
Q2: B) Umpire
Q2: C) Spaniards
Q3: A) Certain or sure
Q3: B) Shortly or soon
Q3: C) Decided

Printed in Great Britain
by Amazon

49063944R00053